Ultimate Tea Recipe Book

Over 100+ Masterful Recipes for the Modern Tea Lover

JULIAN LANGLEY

Copyright

This book is copyright © 2024 by Julian Langley. All rights are reserved. Any unauthorized reproduction, sharing, or distribution of this work, in part or in its entirety, is strictly prohibited. This includes any form of digital or analog replica, such as photocopying, recording, or information storage and retrieval systems, except as permitted under sections of copyright law for brief quotations in a review.

Legal Disclaimer

The material presented in this book is intended for informational purposes only. No warranty, express or implied, on the quality, precision, or suitability for a particular purpose of the content is offered. The author shall not be held responsible for any direct, consequential, or incidental damages arising from using or misusing any information herein. While every effort has been made to ensure the accuracy of the material in this book, neither the author nor the publisher accepts responsibility for any mistakes, inaccuracies, or omissions. If you need professional advice, please consult a qualified professional.

Your purchase and use of this book indicate your acceptance of these terms and conditions.

Table of content

Introduction — 5
  The Universal Language of Tea — 6
  Health and Pleasure in Every Cup — 7

Tea Essentials — 8
  A Brief History of Tea — 9
  The Tea Plant: Camellia Sinensis — 10
  The Five Main Types of Tea — 11
    Black Tea — 12
    Green Tea — 13
    White Tea — 14
    Oolong Tea — 15
    Pu-erh Tea — 16
  Loose Leaf vs. Tea Bags: A Comparison — 17
  Storing Tea for Freshness and Flavor — 18

The Alchemy of Tea Brewing — 19
  The Perfect Water: Source and Temperature — 20
  Timing the Steep: Guidelines for Perfection — 21
  Tools of the Trade: Essential Tea Accessories — 22
  Enhancing Flavors:
  Natural Sweeteners and Spices — 23

A World of Tea Recipes — 24
  Breakfast Teas: Energize Your Morning — 24
    Sunrise Citrus Black Tea — 25
    Morning Glory Green Tea — 25
    Mint Awakening Herbal Blend — 26
    Spiced Assam Chai — 26
    Earl Grey with a Twist of Bergamot — 27
    Lively Lemon Ginger Detox Tea — 27
    Matcha Energy Booster — 28
    Sweet Cinnamon Oolong Revival — 28
    Peppermint Pick-Me-Up — 29
    Honey Vanilla Rooibos Delight — 29
    Golden Turmeric and Black Pepper Tea — 30
    Jasmine Dawn Elixir — 30
    Berry Blast White Tea Infusion — 31
    Zesty Orange Pekoe Punch — 31
    Ginseng and Green Tea Power Brew — 32
    Invigorating Lemongrass Mate — 32
    Cardamom and Clove Morning Tea — 33
    Pomegranate Panache Black Tea — 33
    Refreshing Fennel and Green Tea Blend — 34
    Bold Breakfast Pu-erh — 34
  Afternoon Teas: Refresh and Revitalize — 35
    Apricot Orchard Oolong — 36
    Lavender Breeze Chamomile Infusion — 36
    Peach Perfection White Tea — 37
    Floral Symphony Rose Tea — 37
    Citrus Harmony Earl Grey — 38
    Mint Medley Green Tea — 38
    Raspberry Hibiscus Cooler — 39
    Morning Energizer Darjeeling Tea — 39
    Bergamot Bliss Herbal Tisane — 40
    Caramel Whisper Black Tea — 40
    Summer Berry Sangria Tea — 41
    Jasmine Jewel Green Tea — 41
    Golden Chrysanthemum Brew — 42
    Cherry Blossom Sencha — 42
    Lemon Verbena and Thyme Tonic — 43
    Spiced Orange Rooibos — 43
    Apple Cinnamon Morning Energizer — 44
    Ginger Peach Tea Sparkler — 44
    Vanilla Orchid Oolong — 45
    Moroccan Mint and Licorice Tea — 45
  Evening Teas: Unwind and Relax — 46
    Moonlight Chamomile Dream — 47
    Twilight Lavender Soothe — 47
    Starlight Mint Melody — 48
    Evening Rose Hip Serenade — 48
    Celestial Lemon Balm Calm — 49
    Decaf Ceylon Solace — 49
    Nightfall Valerian Whisper — 50
    Sundown Spiced Vanilla — 50
    Dusk Delight Passionflower — 51
    Milky Way Warm Cinnamon Infusion — 51

Tranquil Tulsi and Orange	52
Restful Rooibos Retreat	52
Serene Sage and Honey Hush	53
After-Dinner Anise Comfort	53
Peaceful Peppermint and Licorice	54
Slumbering Lotus Steep	54
Quiet Time Tangerine Blend	55
Cozy Clove and Cocoa Tisane	55
Sleepy Thyme Embrace	56
Dream Weaver's Wild Berry Brew	56
Dinner Teas: Pairing with Meals	57
Rich Lapsang Souchong Smoky Blend	58
Bold Masala Chai for Spicy Cuisine	58
Delicate White Peony for Light Dishes	59
Savory Sage Green Tea	59
Hearty Roasted Oolong for Grilled Foods	60
Elegant Jasmine Harmony for Asian Fare	60
Zesty Lemon-Ginger Detox for Cleansing	61
Sophisticated Earl Grey for European Cuisine	61
Warming Cinnamon Pu-erh	62
Refreshing Mint and Cucumber Green Tea	62
Floral Hibiscus Bliss for Tropical Meals	63
Robust Yunnan Black Tea for Rich Foods	63
Soothing Lavender Grey for After-Dinner Relaxation	64
Citrus Burst Darjeeling for Seafood	64
Spice Market Herbal Infusion	65
Smoked Cherry Wood Black Tea	65
Artisanal Bergamot and Rose Hip Blend	66
Fragrant Lemongrass and Basil Tisane	66
Sweet Lychee Black Tea for Dessert Pairing	67
Fennel and Anise Digestif Herbal Tea	67
Caramelized Honey Rooibos for Comforting Evenings	68
Vanilla Orchid Black Tea for Sophisticated Palates	68
Special Occasions: Celebratory and Seasonal Teas	69
Festive Winter Spice Tea	70
Spring Cherry Blossom Celebration	70
Summer Solstice Iced Berry Blend	71
Autumn Harvest Pumpkin Chai	71
New Year's Sparkling Tea Toast	72
Valentine's Rose and Chocolate Elixir	72
Mother's Day Floral Bouquet Tea	73
Father's Day Bold Breakfast Blend	73
Halloween Spooky Spearmint Brew	74
Thanksgiving Cranberry-Apple Infusion	74
Christmas Eve Peppermint Twist	75
Easter Morning Honey-Lemon Green Tea	75
Fourth of July Star-Spangled Cooler	76
Hanukkah Blueberry Bliss	76
Diwali Spiced Saffron Tea	77
Midsummer Night's Dream Herbal Mix	77
Autumn Equinox Cider Spice Tea	78
Winter Solstice Gingerbread Tea	78
Spring Renewal Detox Blend	79
Anniversary Romantic Red Rooibos	79
Conclusion	**80**
Index	**81**

Introduction

Embark on a captivating journey into the heart of a beverage that has charmed kings, inspired poets, and soothed millions over centuries. This is an exploration not just of flavors and aromas but of cultures, traditions, and the subtle art that transforms a simple leaf into a cup of magic. Welcome to the enchanting world of tea, where each sip tells a story and every brew is a bridge between the past and the present.

Imagine a world where every leaf has a voice. As you turn these pages, you will hear whispers of ancient forests, bustling marketplaces, serene temples, and elegant parlors. This journey is a celebration of diversity and unity, a testament to how a single plant can mean so many things to different people.

Here, tea is more than a mere drink; it's a ritual, an art, a companion. From the ritualistic brewing methods that demand patience and respect to the simple pleasure of a morning cup that sets the tone for the day, tea encompasses a spectrum of experiences. This exploration is as much about discovering these diverse rituals and traditions as it is about finding your unique connection to this universal beverage.

As we delve into this world, we uncover not just the rich flavors and health benefits that tea offers but also the moments of joy, reflection, and connection it brings. Whether it's a solitary cup that offers solace, a shared pot that fosters friendship, or a ceremonial brew that honors tradition, every aspect of tea is a celebration of life's simple pleasures.

In this journey, we are not just learning how to brew a perfect cup. We are learning to savor moments, to appreciate the subtleties, and to connect with a tradition that spans across borders and generations. So, let us begin this journey with an open heart and an eager palate, ready to experience the myriad wonders that the world of tea has to offer.

The Universal Language of Tea

Tea, in its simplest form, is a conversation between water and leaf, but in its complexity, it's a language that speaks across cultures, transcending geographical and historical boundaries. This universal language of tea is not confined to mere words but is expressed in the aromas, flavors, and rituals that accompany each cup.

From the lush fields of Sri Lanka to the terraced gardens of China, each region whispers its own dialect in this tea language. The robust Assam teas, the delicate Darjeelings, the earthy Pu-erhs, and the floral Oolongs - each variety tells the story of the land it comes from, the climate that nurtured it, and the hands that harvested it. In every sip, one can taste the essence of its origin, a unique terroir that cannot be replicated.

But tea is more than just a beverage; it's a connector of people. The traditional Japanese tea ceremony, the Cha Dao, is not just about drinking tea but about the philosophy of harmony, respect, purity, and tranquility. Similarly, the British afternoon tea is not merely a meal but a social event, a ritual that has become synonymous with comfort and class.

In every corner of the world, tea plays a role in daily life. It's a morning ritual for some, a moment of respite for others. It's a drink that comforts the lonely and enhances social gatherings. Whether it's a family gathering around a samovar in Russia, a group of friends sharing a pot of mint tea in Morocco, or a solitary moment of reflection with a cup of jasmine tea, tea creates a universal bond that resonates with people of all ages and cultures.

The language of tea is also one of health and wellness. It speaks of healing and nourishment, providing a natural medicine for a variety of ailments as well as a source of peace and mindfulness in our often frantic lives. Each type of tea, with its unique antioxidants and medicinal properties, contributes to this dialogue about health, adding another layer to the richness of this beverage.

As you journey through the world of tea, you engage in this universal dialogue. You become part of a tradition that spans thousands of years and countless cultures. Learning the language of tea is not just about understanding different types of teas and their preparations; it's about immersing yourself in a global culture that values connection, wellness, and the simple pleasures of life. It's about discovering that, despite our diverse backgrounds, we can all find common ground over a cup of tea.

Health and Pleasure in Every Cup

As we delve into the world of tea, it's not just the rich tapestry of cultures and traditions that captivate us, but also the remarkable interplay of health and pleasure in every cup. This sublime fusion is what makes tea a beverage revered not only for its taste but also for its myriad health benefits, making each sip a toast to wellbeing.

Tea, in its myriad forms, is a powerhouse of natural goodness. It's more than a pleasant drink; it's a wellness elixir, packed with antioxidants, vitamins, and minerals. Green tea is famous for its potential to enhance metabolism and promote heart health due to its high catechin content. Black tea, known for its robust flavor, also offers benefits for cardiovascular health and stress reduction. Herbal teas, from calming chamomile to invigorating peppermint, offer a spectrum of therapeutic effects, including digestive aid and relaxation.

But the pleasure of tea extends beyond its health benefits. It's found in the warmth of a freshly brewed cup on a cold morning, the soothing aroma that unfurls from a steaming pot, and the first flavorful sip that melts away the day's worries. There's a certain delight in the ritual of tea-making itself – the selection of leaves, the precise temperature of water, the patient steeping – which turns the act of brewing tea into a mindful, meditative process.

Moreover, tea is a versatile companion to every mood and occasion. A brisk morning requires a strong, energizing brew, while a lazy afternoon might call for something light and floral. There's a tea to invigorate, to comfort, to refresh, and to savor. This adaptability is what makes tea a personal experience, one where pleasure is tailored to the individual palate and need.

In a world where the pursuit of health often comes at the cost of pleasure, tea stands out as a delightful exception. It bridges the gap between nurturing the body and delighting the senses. Whether it's through the complex flavors that dance on the tongue or the gentle calm that envelops the mind, tea offers a holistic experience that nourishes both the body and the soul.

In this subchapter, we celebrate not just tea as a beverage, but as a symbol of balanced living. Each cup is a reminder that taking care of oneself can be a joyful, indulgent experience. So, as we explore the world of tea, let us savor not just the flavors and aromas, but also the profound sense of wellbeing that comes with every brewed cup.

Tea Essentials

A Brief History of Tea

The story of tea is as rich and complex as the drink itself, woven into the fabric of countless cultures over thousands of years. This brief history takes us on a journey through time and across continents, tracing the evolution of tea from an ancient medicinal brew to a global phenomenon.

Tea's journey from China to the rest of the world is a tale of trade, cultural exchange, and even espionage. During the Tang Dynasty (618-907 CE), tea was a symbol of sophistication and societal status in Chinese society. The art of tea-making was refined, and it became integral to Chinese culture and ceremonies. The famous work "The Classic of Tea" by Lu Yu during this period is a testament to the significance of tea in Chinese culture.

The introduction of tea to the West is marked by intrigue and colonial ambition. In the 16th century, Portuguese traders and missionaries encountered tea in China and brought it back to Europe. However, it was the Dutch who first commercialized tea in Europe in the early 17th century. The drink quickly became popular among European aristocracy, especially in Britain, where it would eventually become a national obsession.

The origins of tea are steeped in legend and antiquity, with the earliest references dating back to ancient China. According to legend, the Chinese Emperor Shen Nong discovered tea in 2737 BCE when leaves from a wild tree drifted into his pot of boiling water, creating an aromatic infusion. What began as a medicinal concoction soon transformed into a daily beverage, celebrated for both its flavors and health benefits.

Tea spread to other countries of Asia, such as Japan and Korea, thanks to Buddhist monks who traveled to China and returned with tea seeds and leaves. In Japan, tea became a central part of Zen Buddhism and evolved into the Japanese tea ceremony, a spiritual and aesthetic ritual for preparing and drinking matcha, a powdered green tea.

The British were essential in the global tea tale, particularly in tea planting in their colonies. In order to break China's tea monopoly, the British East India Company initiated large-scale tea production in India in the nineteenth century. The discovery and development of tea plantations in Assam and later in Darjeeling and Ceylon (now Sri Lanka) transformed the global tea industry.

Tea's history is also marked by darker chapters, including its role in the Opium Wars between Britain and China and the exploitative conditions in colonial tea plantations. However, as tea plantations spread to Africa and other parts of the world, the industry gradually evolved, with a growing focus on sustainability and fair trade practices in recent times.

Today, tea is the second most consumed beverage in the world after water, a testament to its enduring appeal. Its history reflects not just the spread of a beverage, but the exchange of culture, the interplay of economics and politics, and the shared human experience. In every cup of tea, we drink a small part of this vast and fascinating history.

The Tea Plant: Camellia Sinensis

At the heart of every variety of tea lies a single, unifying element: the tea plant, Camellia sinensis. Understanding this remarkable plant is key to appreciating the diversity and richness of tea. This subchapter explores the botany, cultivation, and varieties of Camellia sinensis, shedding light on how this one species gives rise to the multitude of teas enjoyed around the world.

Born in East Asia, Camellia sinensis is presently cultivated in tropical and subtropical regions worldwide as a species of evergreen shrub or small tree. The plant's leaves and leaf buds are used to produce tea. The character of tea, ranging from subtle and delicate to robust and pungent, is determined by the variety of the plant, the environment in which it's grown, and the methods used for processing its leaves.

Camellia sinensis var. sinensis and Camellia sinensis var. assamica are the two principal varieties of the Camellia sinensis plant that are cultivated for tea. The former, often referred to as Chinese tea, is a smaller-leafed variety that thrives in cooler climates and is known for its wide range of flavors and aromas. It is typically used to produce white, green, and certain black teas. The latter, known as Assam tea, features larger leaves and is native to the Assam region in India. It is well-suited to warmer climates and is commonly used for robust, malty black teas.

The cultivation of tea is an art that requires knowledge, patience, and a deep connection to the land. Tea plants are typically grown in terraced gardens or estates, where they can be carefully managed for optimum quality. Aspects such as precipitation, altitude, climate, and soil composition all significantly influence the ultimate flavor profile of the tea.

Harvesting tea is a meticulous process, often done by hand to ensure the integrity of the leaves. The timing and method of harvesting have a profound impact on the tea's flavor. For instance, the first flush — the first picking of the year — is highly prized for its fresh, vibrant flavors. The leaves are usually plucked early in the day to preserve their quality and are then processed through various methods like withering, rolling, oxidizing, and drying to create different types of tea.

Each step in the processing of tea leaves, from plucking to packaging, contributes to the unique characteristics of the final product. For example, green tea is minimally oxidized, preserving its green color and fresh, grassy flavor. Black tea, on the other hand, is fully oxidized, resulting in a darker leaf color and a richer, more robust flavor profile. Camellia sinensis is more than just a plant; it's the foundation of a global phenomenon that touches cultures, economies, and individuals. By understanding the nature and nuances of this plant, tea enthusiasts can deepen their appreciation for each cup they savor. From its leaf to your teapot, Camellia sinensis is a symbol of the complexity and diversity of the world of tea.

The Five Main Types of Tea

Black Tea

Black Tea: Robust and full-bodied, black tea is the most oxidized, giving it a bold, rich flavor and higher caffeine content. Often enjoyed with milk or lemon, it's perfect for a morning boost or an afternoon pick-me-up.

Green Tea

Green Tea: Known for its delicate flavors and health benefits, green tea is minimally oxidized. It offers a fresh, grassy taste with subtle floral notes and is packed with antioxidants, making it a popular choice for wellness enthusiasts.

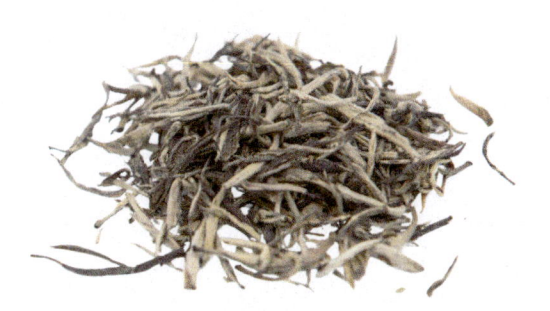

White Tea

White Tea: The most delicate of all teas, white tea is prized for its light, subtle flavor profile. It's made from young leaves and buds, offering a sweet, silky taste, and is known for its antioxidant properties and lower caffeine levels.

Oolong Tea

Oolong Tea: Oolong tea, partially oxidized, stands between green and black tea, offering a diverse range of flavors - from light and floral to dark and toasty. Its complexity is revered by connoisseurs, and it's often appreciated for its digestive benefits.

Pu-erh Tea

Pu-erh Tea: A unique type of fermented tea from China, Pu-erh is known for its earthy, deep flavors that evolve with age. It's highly valued for its digestive benefits and is often consumed after heavy meals to aid in digestion.

Black Tea

Black tea, known for its powerful flavors and rich history, is the most popular form of tea worldwide. Its journey from the tender green leaves of the Camellia sinensis plant to the robust and aromatic beverage we savor is one of transformation and depth.

Characteristics of Black Tea

Black tea is distinguished by its full-bodied flavor and deep, dark color, a result of the complete oxidation process the leaves undergo. Unlike green or white teas, black tea leaves are allowed to oxidize fully before they are dried, which intensifies their flavor and color. This oxidation process also contributes to the development of black tea's distinct malty, fruity, or even smoky notes, depending on the variety and region of cultivation.

Health Benefits

Apart from its rich flavor, black tea is also appreciated for its health benefits. It contains antioxidants such as theaflavins and thearubigins, which have been linked to a variety of health advantages such as improved heart health and decreased cholesterol levels. Additionally, its moderate caffeine content makes it a stimulating yet balanced choice for a morning or afternoon boost.

Brewing Black Tea

To fully appreciate black tea, proper brewing is key. Typically, black tea is steeped in boiling water (about 212°F or 100°C) for 3 to 5 minutes. This allows the flavors to fully develop while avoiding bitterness. By altering the steeping period, you can adjust the strength of the brew to your liking.

Varieties and Flavors

The world of black tea is vast and varied, with each region offering its unique twist. Assam tea from India is known for its bold, malty flavor, making it a popular choice for breakfast blends. Darjeeling, also from India, offers a more delicate, muscatel flavor, often described as the 'champagne of teas.' Ceylon tea from Sri Lanka is prized for its rich and strong flavors, often with hints of chocolate or spice. Chinese black teas, like Keemun, are known for their smooth, slightly smoky taste.

Cultural Significance

Black tea holds a significant place in many cultures. In Britain, it is synonymous with the traditional tea time, often enjoyed with milk and sugar. In the Middle East, black tea is a symbol of hospitality, frequently served sweet and strong. In the United States, iced black tea is a staple in the South, reflecting a regional adaptation of the classic beverage.

Green Tea

Green tea, characterized by its delicate flavors and myriad health benefits, is a testament to the art of preservation in tea processing. Green tea, unlike black tea, is not oxidized, allowing it to retain its green color and a profile rich in subtle, fresh flavors and antioxidants.

Brewing Green Tea

The brewing of green tea is a delicate process. It typically requires cooler water (around 175°F or 80°C) and a shorter steeping time (1-3 minutes) compared to black tea. This prevents the extraction of excessive bitterness and allows the gentle flavors to shine through.

Processing and Minimal Oxidation

The key to green tea's delicate character lies in its processing. Following harvest, the tea leaves are swiftly cooked by steaming (as in Japan) or pan-firing (as in China). This crucial step halts the oxidation process, preserving the green color and delicate flavor compounds of the leaves. Following this, the leaves are rolled into various shapes - a step that contributes not only to the aesthetic but also to the flavor nuances of the tea.

Cultural and Health Aspects

Green tea holds a significant place in many Asian cultures, particularly in China and Japan, where it is integral to tea ceremonies and daily life. The cultural importance of green tea is mirrored in the care taken in its cultivation and brewing.

Health-wise, green tea is a powerhouse of antioxidants, notably catechins like EGCG, which are linked to numerous health benefits. These include improved brain function, fat loss, a lower risk of heart disease, and potential anti-cancer properties. The presence of L-theanine, an amino acid, along with caffeine in green tea, offers a unique combination that improves brain function and induces a more balanced form of alertness compared to other caffeinated beverages.

Flavor Profile and Varieties

Green tea is celebrated for its diverse range of flavors, which can vary from grassy and vegetal to sweet and nutty. Some of the renowned varieties include:

- **Sencha**: A popular Japanese green tea, Sencha offers a balanced blend of sweetness and astringency, with a fresh, grassy aroma.
- **Dragon Well (Longjing)**: Hailing from China, this tea is known for its gentle, sweet flavor and the chestnut overtones.
- **Matcha**: A unique powdered green tea used in traditional Japanese tea ceremonies, Matcha is rich, creamy, and slightly bitter.

White Tea

White tea, known for its subtle delicacy and refined elegance, represents the most minimally processed form of tea. This gentle handling preserves the natural characteristics of the tea leaves, resulting in a light, often sweet brew that is cherished by connoisseurs and casual drinkers alike.

Minimal Processing and Gentle Flavors

The hallmark of white tea lies in its simple, yet precise, processing. It involves very little manipulation - the leaves are plucked and allowed to wither naturally, often in sunlight. This natural withering process allows for minimal oxidation, retaining the soft, natural flavors of the leaves and their silvery-white hairs, which give this tea its name.

Varieties and Taste Profile

White tea offers a spectrum of subtle flavors, characterized by mild, sweet, and delicate notes. Some of the most esteemed varieties of white tea include:

- **Silver Needle (Bai Hao Yin Zhen)**: Consisting only of the top unopened buds, Silver Needle is prized for its smooth, light, and sweet flavor with hints of honey and melon.
- **White Peony (Bai Mu Dan)**: This tea includes both buds and young leaves, offering a fuller flavor than Silver Needle, with floral and fruity undertones.

Brewing White Tea

Brewing white tea is an exercise in restraint. It requires lower water temperatures (around 160°F to 185°F or 70°C to 85°C) and shorter steeping times compared to other teas. This gentle brewing method helps to extract the delicate flavors without overpowering the subtle nuances of the tea.

Varieties and Taste Profile

White tea is deeply rooted in Chinese tea culture, often associated with sophistication and tranquility. Historically reserved for royalty, it is a symbol of elegance and respect.

From a health perspective, white tea is a treasure trove of benefits. Being the least processed, it retains a high level of antioxidants, particularly polyphenols, which contribute to its health-promoting properties. These include potential anti-aging effects, cardiovascular health support, and assistance in lowering the risk of chronic diseases. Its relatively low caffeine content also makes it a gentle choice for those sensitive to caffeine.

Oolong Tea

Oolong tea, with its diverse range and nuanced profile, occupies a unique position in the tea world, bridging the gap between green and black teas. This semi-oxidized tea is celebrated for its complex flavors and aromatic qualities, which vary widely depending on the degree of oxidation and the crafting techniques employed.

Semi-Oxidation and Versatile Flavors

The defining characteristic of oolong tea is its partial oxidation, which can range from about 10% to 70%. This controlled oxidation process, coupled with meticulous crafting techniques, gives rise to a spectrum of flavors and aromas, from light and floral to dark and full-bodied. The leaves are often rolled into distinctive shapes, such as tight balls or long, curly leaves, which unfurl during brewing, releasing their flavor profile.

Notable Varieties

Oolong tea offers a rich tapestry of styles and flavors. Some notable varieties include:
- Tieguanyin: A popular variety from China's Fujian Province, known for its floral, creamy, and smooth taste.
- Da Hong Pao (Big Red Robe): A highly prized oolong from the Wuyi Mountains, with a rich, roasted flavor and a hint of spice.
- High Mountain Oolong: Grown in Taiwan's high-altitude regions, these oolongs are known for their crisp, floral, and subtly sweet flavors.

Brewing Oolong Tea

The brewing of oolong tea is a nuanced art. Typically, it requires water that's just below boiling (around 185°F to 205°F or 85°C to 96°C) and a steeping time of 1 to 5 minutes, depending on the specific variety. Oolong teas can often be re-steeped multiple times, with each infusion revealing a different aspect of the tea's flavor profile.

Cultural Richness and Health Aspects

In Chinese and Taiwanese tea traditions, oolong tea is commonly connected with traditional tea rituals and gongfu tea brewing, a practice that stresses the skill and artistry of tea preparation.

When it comes to health advantages, oolong tea is high in antioxidants, vitamins, and minerals. Its partial oxidation results in a unique composition of theaflavins, thearubigins, and catechins, which are believed to contribute to various health benefits such as aiding in weight management, improving heart health, and supporting digestion.

Pu-erh Tea

Pu-erh tea, a unique category hailing from Yunnan Province in China, stands apart in the tea world for its distinctive aging process and deep, earthy flavors. This fermented tea, known for its health benefits and complex taste profile, offers a tea experience that is both ancient and dynamic.

Fermentation and Aging

What sets pu-erh tea apart is its fermentation process. Unlike other teas, pu-erh undergoes a microbial fermentation after the leaves are dried and rolled. This process can continue for months, years, or even decades, contributing to the tea's evolving flavor and character. Pu-erh tea is available in two types: Sheng (raw) and Shou (ripe). Sheng pu-erh slowly ferments and matures over time, while Shou pu-erh is rapidly fermented, giving it a more immediate earthy quality.

Brewing Pu-erh Tea

The brewing of pu-erh tea is an art in itself. It typically requires boiling water, and the tea can withstand multiple steepings, with each infusion revealing different nuances of flavor. The initial steeping is often brief and discarded, a step known as 'rinsing,' which helps to awaken the flavors of the tea.

Character and Varieties

Pu-erh tea is renowned for its rich, earthy, and sometimes woody or smoky flavors. The flavor varies widely depending on age, processing method, and storage circumstances. Older pu-erh teas are highly valued for their smoothness and depth of flavor. The tea is often pressed into cakes or bricks, which, apart from being practical for storage and aging, have become a distinct feature of pu-erh tea presentation.

Cultural Significance and Health Benefits

Pu-erh tea holds a special place in Chinese tea culture, revered not just for its taste but also for its traditional value. It is often consumed as a digestive aid and is believed to have detoxifying properties.

Pu-erh tea is recognized for its ability to aid in weight loss, lower cholesterol levels, and enhance intestinal health due to the presence of beneficial bacteria created during fermentation. Its antioxidant properties are also believed to contribute to overall wellness, including heart health and blood sugar regulation.

Loose Leaf vs. Tea Bags: A Comparison

When it comes to enjoying a cup of tea, one of the fundamental choices a tea drinker faces is between loose leaf tea and tea bags. This choice is not just about convenience; it also significantly impacts the flavor, quality, and overall tea experience. Understanding the differences between these two forms of tea is key to selecting the right type for your taste and lifestyle.

Loose Leaf Tea: Quality and Flavor

Loose leaf tea is made up of whole or big tea leaves. One of its primary advantages is the quality of the tea. Loose leaf tea is often made from the finest buds and leaves, resulting in a richer and more complex flavor profile. As the leaves infuse in hot water, they fully expand (a process known as "the agony of the leaves"), allowing all their flavors and aromas to be released.

Loose leaf teas also offer a wider variety in terms of types and flavors, providing more options for exploration to tea enthusiasts. Additionally, they can be steeped multiple times, with each infusion revealing different notes and depths of flavor, making it a more economical and environmentally friendly option over time.

Tea Bags: Convenience and Consistency

Tea bags, on the other hand, are known for their convenience and uniformity. They typically contain smaller pieces of leaves or tea dust, which allows for a quick and consistent brew. This can be particularly appealing for those with a busy lifestyle or for those who prefer a consistent taste in every cup.

However, the small size of the tea particles in bags can often lead to a more rapid release of tannins, resulting in a more astringent brew. Additionally, the space within tea bags can be limiting for the leaves to expand, which can affect the infusion process and the tea's flavor complexity.

Environmental Considerations

From an environmental standpoint, loose leaf tea is often seen as a more sustainable option. It generally involves less packaging and waste compared to individually wrapped tea bags. However, many tea companies are now offering biodegradable or compostable tea bags as a more eco-friendly alternative.

Quality vs. Convenience

In summary, the choice between loose leaf tea and tea bags often comes down to a trade-off between quality and convenience. Loose leaf tea provides a more realistic and nuanced tea experience, making it excellent for individuals who appreciate the ritual of brewing and appreciating their tea. Tea bags, with their ease of use and consistent results, cater to those seeking a quick, convenient, and uniform cup of tea.

Both styles have advantages and disadvantages, and the choice for one over the other might vary depending on personal preference, lifestyle, and the occasion. Understanding these differences allows tea drinkers to make more informed choices and enjoy their tea to the fullest.

Storing Tea for Freshness and Flavor

Proper storage of tea is essential in preserving its freshness, flavor, and health benefits. Tea, being a delicate product, is susceptible to a variety of environmental factors that can degrade its quality. Understanding how to store tea correctly can greatly enhance your tea experience by ensuring each cup retains the full character and taste intended by the tea maker.

Protecting Tea from the Elements

Tea's greatest enemies are air, moisture, light, and strong odors. Exposure to these factors can cause the tea's natural oils and aromatic compounds to degrade, resulting in a stale or bland cup.

- Air and Moisture: Oxygen can accelerate the degradation of tea, while moisture can lead to mold growth. To avoid exposure to air and moisture, tea should be stored in airtight containers.
- Light: Tea can fade and lose flavor if exposed to direct sunshine or intense light. Tea should be stored in opaque or dark-colored containers to protect it from light.
- Odors: Tea leaves are extremely absorbent and can readily absorb the scents and aromas of their environment. Store tea away from strong-smelling foods or substances.

Choosing the Right Container

The ideal container for storing tea is airtight, opaque, and made of materials that do not impart any flavor to the tea, such as tin, ceramic, or dark glass. Avoid plastic or paper containers, as they may not provide an adequate seal and can impart unwanted flavors.

Temperature and Humidity Considerations

Tea should be kept in a cool, dry location. Excessive heat can hasten the degradation of tea, while high humidity can encourage mold growth. Tea should not be stored in the refrigerator or freezer because condensation can introduce moisture into the tea. However, for some teas like green teas, which are more sensitive to temperature and light, cooler storage may be beneficial.

Organizing and Labeling

If you have a variety of teas, it's important to organize and label them clearly. This not only helps in easily finding the tea you want but also in tracking the freshness and shelf life. Each container should be labeled with the type of tea and the date of purchase.

Shelf Life of Tea

While tea does not spoil in the same way as food, it does lose its flavor over time. The shelf life of tea depends on the type and how well it is stored. Generally, black teas last longer than green or white teas. A well-stored tea can maintain its quality for up to a year, though it's usually best consumed within a few months of purchase.

The Alchemy of Tea Brewing

The Perfect Water: Source and Temperature

In the alchemy of brewing tea, water plays a pivotal role. It is not just a solvent but a co-creator of the taste, aroma, and color of the tea. The quality of water and its temperature are fundamental in extracting the full potential of tea leaves, making the choice of water and its heating an art in itself.

Water Quality: The Foundation of Flavor

The purity and composition of water significantly affect the taste of tea. Water with high levels of minerals (hard water) can overpower the delicate flavors of tea, while overly soft water can result in a flat brew. Ideally, fresh, filtered, or bottled spring water with a neutral pH and balanced mineral content is preferred. This kind of water complements the tea, allowing its flavors and aromas to shine through without any interference.

The Role of Temperature

Each type of tea requires a different water temperature to maximize flavor release. Using water that is too hot or too cold can drastically alter the tea's taste, making understanding temperature nuances crucial.

Black and Herbal Teas: These robust teas require higher temperatures to fully extract their flavors. Water just off the boil (around 208°F to 212°F or 98°C to 100°C) is ideal.

Oolong Teas: Oolong teas often require a medium range of temperatures. Water around 185°F to 205°F (85°C to 96°C) is generally suitable, depending on the specific type of oolong.

Green and White Teas: These delicate teas are best brewed with cooler water to avoid bitterness. Temperatures around 160°F to 185°F (70°C to 85°C) are recommended.

Heating Water to the Correct Temperature

Achieving the correct water temperature can be done with a kitchen thermometer or a variable temperature kettle. An alternative method is to observe the water's boiling stages, which can provide visual cues: for example, smaller bubbles for green tea temperatures and a full, rolling boil for black tea.

Avoiding Reboiled Water

Using freshly drawn water is important, as reboiling can deplete the oxygen levels in the water, leading to a flat-tasting tea. Each brew should start with fresh, cold water that's brought to temperature.

The Impact of Water on Tea's Chemistry

The temperature and quality of water don't just affect taste but also influence the chemical components extracted from tea leaves, such as caffeine, antioxidants, and essential oils. The right water brings out a balance of these components, contributing to both the flavor and health benefits of the tea.

The perfect water for brewing tea is a harmonious blend of quality, purity, and temperature. By paying attention to these aspects, the tea drinker can enhance the sensory experience of tea, transforming each cup into a perfect expression of flavor and aroma.

Timing the Steep: Guidelines for Perfection

The art of brewing tea is a delicate balance, and timing is a crucial element in this dance of flavors. Steeping tea for the right amount of time is essential to extract the perfect harmony of flavor, aroma, and color. Too short, and the tea will be weak and underdeveloped; too long, and it may turn bitter and overpowering. This subchapter provides guidelines to master the timing of your steep for each type of tea, ensuring every cup reaches its full potential.

General Steeping Guidelines

While personal choice influences the appropriate steeping time, there are broad standards for many types of tea:

- **Black Tea**: Steep for 3-5 minutes. Black tea is robust and can handle longer steeping times, which allow its bold and rich flavors to fully develop.
- **Green Tea**: Steep for 1-3 minutes. Green tea is delicate; a shorter steeping time will prevent the release of too many tannins, which can make the tea taste bitter.
- **White Tea**: Steep for 2-4 minutes. White tea, being subtle in flavor, benefits from a slightly longer steep than green tea, allowing its gentle, nuanced notes to emerge.
- **Oolong Tea**: Steep for 2-5 minutes. Oolong teas vary widely in oxidation, so steeping times can vary. Lighter oolongs generally need less time, while darker ones can be steeped longer.
- **Herbal Tea**: Steep for 5-7 minutes. Herbal teas, made from herbs, spices, and fruits, often require longer steeping times to fully extract their flavors.

Factors Influencing Steeping Time

Several factors can influence the proper steeping period, including:

- **Tea Leaf Size**: Smaller leaves or broken leaves infuse more quickly than whole leaves.
- **Water Temperature**: Higher temperatures can extract flavors more rapidly, potentially reducing steeping time.
- **Personal Taste**: Some prefer a stronger, more robust cup, while others may enjoy a lighter, subtler flavor.

Re-Steeping Tea

Many high-quality teas, especially loose-leaf varieties, can be steeped multiple times. Each subsequent steeping reveals new facets of the tea's flavor profile. Generally, each additional steep should be slightly longer than the previous one.

The Role of Patience and Observation

Steeping tea is not just a matter of timing; it's an exercise in patience and observation. Watching the color of the tea develop, smelling the aromas, and even tasting the tea at different intervals can be part of the personal ritual to find your perfect brew.

Experimentation and Refinement

Mastering the timing of your tea's steep is a fundamental aspect of brewing the perfect cup. By following these guidelines and being mindful of the factors that influence steeping, you can elevate your tea experience, ensuring each cup is a reflection of your personal taste and the tea's intrinsic qualities.

Tools of the Trade: Essential Tea Accessories

Brewing tea is both a science and an art, and like any good craftsman, a tea enthusiast needs the right tools to craft the perfect cup. The world of tea accessories is vast, but there are essential items that can significantly enhance the tea brewing experience. This subchapter introduces the key accessories that are integral to the alchemy of tea brewing, each serving a specific purpose in the ritual of making tea.

Teapots and Kettles

Teapots: The centerpiece of tea brewing, teapots come in various materials like ceramic, glass, porcelain, or cast iron. Each material has its own influence on the tea's flavor. For instance, a clay teapot can absorb flavors over time, adding depth to future brews.

Kettles: A good kettle, preferably one with temperature control for precision brewing, is crucial. Whether electric or stovetop, a kettle that can heat water to the desired temperature is key for extracting the best flavor from tea.

Tea Infusers and Strainers

Infusers: Essential for brewing loose leaf tea, they come in various shapes and sizes. The most common types include metal or silicone infusers, basket-style infusers (which sit inside the rim of the teapot or mug), and tea balls. The key is to choose an infuser that gives the leaves enough room to expand and release their full flavor.

Strainers: Typically made of metal mesh, strainers are used when pouring tea from a teapot to catch any loose leaves. They can be handheld or fit over the top of a cup. Some are fine enough to strain out even the smallest tea particles.

Tea Cups and Mugs

The material and shape of a tea cup or mug can influence the tea's temperature retention and taste perception. Porcelain and bone china are popular for their heat-retention properties and delicate feel. Glass cups are great for enjoying the color of the tea, and ceramic mugs provide a sturdy, heat-retaining option for everyday use.

Measuring Tools

Accurate measurement ensures consistency in tea strength and flavor. Tea spoons or scoops are designed to measure the perfect amount of tea leaves for each cup. Some are specifically sized for different types of tea (e.g., a scoop for green tea may be smaller than one for oolong).

Tea Caddies and Storage Containers

Essential for maintaining the freshness and flavor of tea. Tea caddies are traditionally made of tin or ceramic and provide an airtight seal. Modern options include vacuum-sealed containers. Containers should be opaque to protect tea from light and stored in a cool, dry place.

Tea Trays and Cast Iron Stands

Tea trays are used to organize and display tea accessories and catch any spills. They can be made from bamboo, wood, or metal. Cast iron stands are often used with cast iron teapots and can be decorative as well as functional, protecting surfaces from heat.

Thermometers and Timers

Thermometers help in achieving the correct water temperature for different types of tea. Digital or analog thermometers can be used. Timers ensure tea is steeped for the right amount of time, crucial for achieving the desired flavor.

Enhancing Flavors: Natural Sweeteners and Spices

While tea can be delightful on its own, the addition of natural sweeteners and spices can transform it into an even more flavorful and aromatic beverage. These enhancers not only complement the intrinsic flavors of the tea but also add their own unique profiles, creating a more complex and satisfying sensory experience. This subchapter explores various natural sweeteners and spices that can be used to elevate the flavors of tea.

Natural Sweeteners

Honey: A popular choice for tea, honey adds a natural sweetness along with its own subtle floral notes. Its flavor can vary depending on the flowers from which the bees collected nectar, allowing for interesting pairings with different types of tea.

Maple Syrup: Offering a rich, caramel-like sweetness, maple syrup is an excellent sweetener for stronger teas. It's particularly complementary to black and chai teas.

Agave Nectar: A milder sweetener with a smooth texture, agave nectar dissolves easily in both hot and cold teas, making it a versatile choice for any tea blend.

Spices

Cinnamon: With its warm, sweet, and woody flavor, cinnamon can add depth and warmth to tea, especially to black and chai blends.

Ginger: Known for its spicy kick and health benefits, ginger pairs well with green tea, herbal blends, and is a key ingredient in traditional masala chai.

Cardamom: This aromatic spice, with its sweet, floral, and spicy notes, is a staple in chai recipes and can add a refreshing aroma to black and oolong teas.

Cloves and Star Anise: These spices bring a strong, warm flavor, suitable for robust teas. Cloves and star anise are often used in chai and spiced tea blends.

Citrus Peels and Zests

Adding citrus peels, like lemon or orange, to tea can impart a refreshing, tangy flavor. The zest from these fruits adds a bright note to both black and green teas, enhancing their natural flavors without overpowering them.

Herbs

Mint: Fresh or dried mint leaves can add a cooling, refreshing quality to tea, particularly well-suited to green and herbal teas.

Lavender: Known for its soothing aroma, lavender can lend a floral, slightly sweet note to teas, creating a relaxing and aromatic brew.

Vanilla

A vanilla pod or a few drops of natural vanilla extract can add a creamy, sweet dimension to tea, especially black and dessert teas.

When experimenting with these enhancers, it's important to consider the type of tea and its flavor profile. The key is to achieve a balance where the sweeteners and spices complement, rather than overpower, the natural flavors of the tea. Whether seeking to sweeten, spice, or add a hint of citrus, these natural enhancers can elevate a simple cup of tea into a rich and nuanced beverage, tailor-made to your taste preferences.

A World of Tea Recipes

Breakfast Teas: Energize Your Morning

SUNRISE CITRUS BLACK TEA

Wake up to the invigorating aroma of this Sunrise Citrus Black Tea, a perfect blend of robust black tea and refreshing citrus flavors to kickstart your morning. It's a delightful fusion that balances the depth of black tea with the bright, uplifting notes of citrus.

Equipment: Teapot, Strainer, Kettle

Ingredients:

- 2 teaspoons black tea leaves (assam or ceylon recommended)
- 1 orange, zest only
- 1 lemon, zest only
- 2 cups water
- honey or sweetener of choice, to taste
- optional: fresh mint leaves for garnish

2 servings

5 minutes

5 minutes

Directions:

1. Boil water in a kettle to about 208°F (98°C) - just below boiling.
2. Place the black tea leaves in the teapot.
3. Add the zest of one orange and one lemon to the teapot. If you prefer a stronger citrus flavor, increase the amount of zest.
4. Pour the hot water over the tea leaves and citrus zest. Allow the tea to steep for 3-5 minutes, depending on your preferred strength.
5. While the tea is steeping, warm your tea cups with a bit of hot water to maintain the tea's temperature when served.
6. After steeping, strain the tea into the warmed cups.
7. Sweeten with honey or your preferred sweetener to taste.
8. If desired, garnish each cup with a fresh mint leaf for an additional refreshing note.

Enjoy yourself

MORNING GLORY GREEN TEA

The Morning Glory Green Tea is an uplifting and refreshing beverage, perfect for starting your day. This recipe combines the gentle, grassy notes of green tea with the bright, invigorating flavors of fresh citrus and a hint of sweet honey, creating a balanced and rejuvenating morning drink.

2 servings   5 minutes   3 minutes

Equipment: Teapot, Strainer, Kettle

Ingredients:

- 2 teaspoons black tea leaves (assam or ceylon recommended)
- 1 orange, zest only
- 1 lemon, zest only
- 2 cups water
- honey or sweetener of choice, to taste
- optional: fresh mint leaves for garnish

Directions:

1. Bring water to a near boil at about 175°F (80°C), then let it cool for a minute. This temperature is ideal for green tea, as too hot water can make it bitter.
2. Place green tea leaves in the teapot.
3. Fill the kettle halfway with fresh orange and lemon juice.
4. Pour the slightly cooled water over the tea leaves and juice. Allow it to steep for about 3 minutes. Oversteeping can make green tea taste bitter.
5. In the meantime, warm your tea cups by swirling a bit of hot water in them, then discard the water.
6. After steeping, strain the tea into the warmed cups.
7. Stir in honey to sweeten, adjusting according to taste.
8. If desired, garnish each cup with a thin slice of orange and lemon for added aroma and visual appeal.

MINT AWAKENING HERBAL BLEND

The Mint Awakening Herbal Blend is a revitalizing and refreshing tea, perfect for jump-starting your morning. This vibrant blend combines the invigorating freshness of mint with subtle hints of citrus and sweetness, making it an ideal drink to awaken your senses.

Equipment: Teapot, Kettle, Strainer

Ingredients:

- 2 tablespoons fresh mint leaves, finely chopped
- 1 teaspoon dried lemon balm
- 1/2 teaspoon dried chamomile flowers
- 2 cups boiling water
- 1 tablespoon honey, or to taste
- optional: lemon slices for garnish

2 servings
5 minutes
10 minutes

Directions:

1. Boil water in a kettle.
2. Combine the fresh mint leaves, dried lemon balm, and chamomile flowers in the teapot.
3. Once the water has reached a rolling boil, pour it over the herb mixture in the teapot.
4. Allow the tea to steep for about 6-10 minutes. The longer you steep, the stronger the mint flavor will be.
5. While the tea is steeping, warm your tea cups with a bit of hot water, then discard the water.
6. After steeping, strain the tea into the warmed cups.
7. Sweeten with honey to your liking.
8. If desired, garnish each cup with a lemon slice for an extra zing.

Tea time

SPICED ASSAM CHAI

Spiced Assam Chai is a robust and aromatic tea, perfect for a stimulating start to your morning. This traditional Indian chai combines the bold flavor of Assam tea with a warming blend of spices, creating a rich and comforting beverage.

4 servings   10 minutes   20 minutes

Equipment: Saucepan, Strainer

Ingredients:

- 4 cups water
- 4 teaspoons assam tea leaves
- 2 cinnamon sticks
- 4 green cardamom pods, crushed
- 4 cloves
- 1-inch piece of fresh ginger, sliced
- 1/2 cup milk
- 2-4 tablespoons sugar, or to taste

Directions:

1. Bring water to a boil in a saucepan.
2. Add the Assam tea leaves, cinnamon sticks, crushed cardamom pods, cloves, and sliced ginger to the boiling water.
3. Bake for 10 to 15 minutes while reducing the heat. The longer you simmer, the stronger the spice flavors will be.
4. Add milk and sugar to the saucepan. Bring the mixture back to a boil.
5. Reduce the temperature and simmer for an additional five minutes, after it has boiled.
6. Strain the chai into cups or a teapot, ensuring to remove all the spices and tea leaves.
7. Taste and adjust sugar if necessary.

EARL GREY WITH A TWIST OF BERGAMOT

This Earl Grey with a Twist of Bergamot is a classic tea with a citrusy upgrade, perfect for an energizing morning. The traditional flavor of Earl Grey is enhanced with a fresh twist of bergamot, offering a unique and aromatic experience.

Equipment: Teapot, Strainer, Kettle

Ingredients:

- 2 teaspoons earl grey tea leaves
- 1 fresh bergamot orange, zest and juice
- 2 cups boiling water
- optional: honey or sugar, to taste
- optional: thin bergamot orange slices for garnish

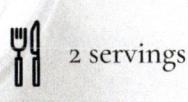

2 servings

5 minutes

5 minutes

Directions:

1. Boil water in the kettle to about 208°F (98°C).
2. Place the Earl Grey tea leaves in the teapot.
3. Zest the bergamot orange and add the zest to the teapot. Be careful to avoid the white pith as it can be bitter.
4. Slice the bergamot orange in half and squeeze a bit of its juice into the teapot for an extra citrusy flavor.
5. Pour out the hot water over the tea leaves and bergamot zest. Allow the tea to steep for about three to five minutes, depending on how strong you prefer your tea.
6. While the tea is steeping, warm your tea cups with a bit of hot water, then discard it.
7. Strain the tea into the warmed cups.
8. If desired, sweeten with sugar or honey to taste.
9. Garnish with a thin slice of bergamot orange, if using.

Zen Sip

LIVELY LEMON GINGER DETOX TEA

Lively Lemon Ginger Detox Tea is a zesty and revitalizing beverage, ideal for energizing your mornings. This tea mixes the spicy warmth of ginger with the refreshing tang of lemon to create a delectable cleansing drink that stimulates the senses.

2 servings   10 minutes   5 minutes

Equipment: Saucepan, Strainer

Ingredients:

- 4 cups water
- 2 tablespoons fresh ginger, thinly sliced
- 1 lemon, juice and zest
- 1 tablespoon honey, or to taste
- optional: a sprinkle of cayenne pepper for added heat
- optional: fresh mint leaves for garnish

Directions:

1. Water is brought to a simmer in a saucepan.
2. Add the thinly sliced ginger and the zest of the lemon to the boiling water.
3. Allow it to percolate for approximately 5 minutes to allow the ginger flavor to infuse.
4. Turn off the heat. To the saucepan, add the freshly strained lemon juice. Stir well.
5. If you're using cayenne pepper, add it now for a spicy touch.
6. Permit the tea to percolate for five minutes longer.
7. Before transferring the tea to cups or a teapot, strain out the lemon zest and ginger slices.
8. Sweeten with honey to your liking. Stir well until the honey is dissolved.
9. If using, garnish each cup with a fresh mint leaf for a refreshing aroma.

MATCHA ENERGY BOOSTER

The Matcha Energy Booster is a vibrant and energizing drink, perfect for a morning lift. This traditional Japanese tea is known for its rich, earthy flavor and numerous health benefits, including sustained energy and focus.

Equipment: Matcha whisk (chasen), Matcha bowl (chawan), Small sieve or sifter

Ingredients:

- 1-2 teaspoons high-quality matcha powder
- 1 cup hot water (about 175°F or 80°C)
- optional: honey or agave syrup, to taste
- optional: a splash of milk or milk alternative for a creamier version

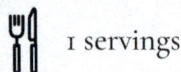

1 servings
5 minutes
5 minutes

Directions:

1. To eliminate any lumps, sift the matcha powder into the matcha vessel. This ensures a smooth tea.
2. Add a small amount of hot water to the matcha powder in the bowl.
3. Using the matcha whisk, whisk briskly in a "W" motion until the tea becomes frothy. This process should take about 1-2 minutes and helps aerate the tea, bringing out its natural sweetness.
4. Once the tea is frothy and bright green, add more hot water to the bowl, adjusting to your preferred strength.
5. If you're sweetening your matcha, add honey or agave syrup at this stage and whisk gently to combine.
6. Add a splash of your choice milk or milk substitute and stir lightly for a creamier version.

Tea Delight

SWEET CINNAMON OOLONG REVIVAL

Elevate your morning with the invigorating aroma and sweet spiced notes of Sweet Cinnamon Oolong Revival. This tea blend combines the complex flavors of oolong with the warming comfort of cinnamon, complemented by a subtle sweetness, for a revitalizing start to your day.

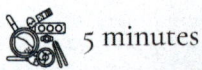

2 servings   5 minutes   7 minutes

Equipment: Teapot, Kettle, Strainer, Teacups

Ingredients:

- 2 teaspoons oolong tea leaves
- 2 cups filtered water
- 1 cinnamon stick
- 2 teaspoons honey, or to taste
- a splash of milk or your preferred milk alternative (optional)
- optional garnish: a sprinkle of ground cinnamon

Directions:

1. Heat the filtered water in a kettle until it reaches about 185°F to 200°F (85-93 °C), just below boiling. Oolong tea is best brewed with slightly cooler water.
2. Place the oolong tea leaves and cinnamon stick into the teapot.
3. Pour out the heated water into the teapot over the tea leaves and cinnamon stick. Allow it to steep for 4 to 7 minutes, depending on how strong you prefer your tea.
4. While the tea is steeping, warm your teacups with a bit of hot water to maintain the temperature of the tea upon serving.
5. After steeping, remove the cinnamon stick and strain the tea into the warmed teacups, using the strainer to catch the leaves.
6. Stir in a teaspoon of honey into each cup, or adjust according to your preferred level of sweetness.
7. For a creamier tea, add a splash of milk or milk alternative and stir well.
8. To add a dash of extra spice, put a pinch of ground cinnamon on top of each cup.
9. Serve immediately and savor the comforting warmth.

PEPPERMINT PICK-ME-UP

Awaken your senses and refresh your morning with the cool and invigorating "Peppermint Pick-Me-Up". This breakfast tea blend combines the bold, stimulating black tea with a splash of zesty peppermint to kickstart your day. It's the perfect accompaniment to any morning routine, offering a balance of natural vigor and soothing warmth.

Equipment: Teapot or saucepan, Strainer or infuser, Measuring spoons

Ingredients:
- 2 cups of water
- 2 tsp black tea leaves, preferably a robust blend like assam or english breakfast
- 1/4 cup fresh peppermint leaves or 2 peppermint tea bags
- 1 tbsp honey (or to taste)
- optional: fresh lemon wedges for serving

2 servings
5 minutes
10 minutes

Directions:
1. In a teapot or saucepan, bring the water to a boil.
2. Reduce the heat to low after adding the black tea leaves to the boiling water. Allow to simmer for 3-4 minutes to extract the full flavor of the tea.
3. Add the peppermint leaves or peppermint tea bags to the pot and continue to simmer for an additional 3-4 minutes. Increase the peppermint steeping time if you prefer a stronger mint flavor.
4. Remove the infuser or sieve the mixture to separate the tea and peppermint leaves from the liquid when it has been removed from the heat.
5. Stir in the honey until completely dissolved. If desired, add more honey to taste.
6. Pour into teacups, and if you like, serve with a fresh lemon wedge to be squeezed into the tea according to individual taste.

Sip Slowly

HONEY VANILLA ROOIBOS DELIGHT

Savor the delicate dance of rich honey with the creamy notes of vanilla as they harmoniously blend with the naturally sweet and herbal flavor of rooibos tea. This Honey Vanilla Rooibos Delight is a comforting, caffeine-free beverage to start your morning with a serene energy and a touch of sweetness.

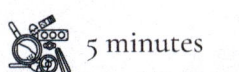

Equipment: Teapot or saucepan, Measuring spoons, Strainer (if using loose leaf tea), Teacups

Ingredients:
- 2 cups water
- 2 tablespoons loose leaf rooibos tea or 2 rooibos tea bags
- 1 vanilla bean pod, split lengthwise and seeds scraped or 1 teaspoon pure vanilla extract
- 2-4 teaspoons honey, to taste
- Milk or milk alternative (optional, for serving)
- Cinnamon stick or ground cinnamon (optional, for garnish)

2 servings
5 minutes
10 minutes

Directions:
1. Thermalize water in a saucepan or teapot until it boils. Meanwhile, prepare your vanilla bean pod by splitting it lengthwise and scraping out the seeds with the back of a knife. If using vanilla extract, have it measured and ready.
2. Reduce the heat after the water reaches a boil and add the loose leaf rooibos tea or tea bags, vanilla bean pod and seeds, or vanilla extract. Allow 7-8 minutes for the tea to steep. The longer you steep, the more profound the flavors will be.
3. Remove the tea from the heat after it has steeped. If you are using loose leaf tea, strain the tea into teacups to remove the leaves and vanilla pod residue. For tea bags, simply remove them from the teacups.
4. Stir in honey while the tea is still warm so it dissolves easily. Depending on your taste, adjust the sweetness.
5. For a velvety enhancement, one may, if they so choose, incorporate a small amount of milk or a milk substitute into the Honey Vanilla Rooibos Delight.
6. As an embellishment, incorporate a small amount of powdered cinnamon or a cinnamon stick to generate a peppery contrast that amplifies the sweetness of the vanilla and honey.

GOLDEN TURMERIC AND BLACK PEPPER TEA

Wake up your senses and invigorate your morning with this bold and aromatic Golden Turmeric and Black Pepper Tea. Turmeric's earthy tones and powerful antioxidants meet a hint of spicy black pepper to increase absorption – a perfect combination to kick-start your day with a touch of warmth.

Equipment: Medium Saucepan, Fine Mesh Strainer, Teacups

Ingredients:
- 2 1/2 cups water
- 2 black tea bags
- 1 tbsp fresh turmeric root, grated (or 1 tsp ground turmeric)
- 1/4 tsp freshly ground black pepper
- 1 tbsp honey, or to taste
- 1 tbsp fresh lemon juice
- optional: milk or milk alternative (for a creamier texture)

1 servings
5 minutes
5 minutes

Directions:
1. Bring the water to a gentle boil in a medium saucepan. Once the water is boiling, reduce the heat to maintain a simmer.
2. Add the black tea bags to the simmering water and let them steep for about 3 minutes.
3. Stir in the grated turmeric root (or ground turmeric) and ground black pepper. Let the mixture simmer for another 5 minutes, allowing the flavors to meld together.
4. Eliminate any particulates from the tea by passing it through a fine mesh strainer after removing the saucepan from the heat.
5. Adjust the sweetness with honey and fresh lemon juice to taste.
6. If preferred, add a splash of milk or a milk substitute to make the tea creamier.
7. Serve the Golden Turmeric and Black Pepper Tea hot in your favorite teacups.

Enjoy yourself

JASMINE DAWN ELIXIR

Embrace the soft light of morning with the Jasmine Dawn Elixir, a delicate and invigorating brew designed to gently awaken the senses. An harmonious blend is achieved when the floral notes of jasmine, the zest of lemon, and the nuanced sweetness of honey are combined. This combination not only invigorates the body but also soothes the spirit.

2 servings   5 minutes   5 minutes

Equipment: Teapot, Strainer, Teacup or Mug

Ingredients:
- 2 teaspoons jasmine green tea leaves
- 2 cups filtered water
- 1 teaspoon lemon juice
- 2 teaspoons honey, or to taste
- optional: fresh jasmine flowers for garnish

Directions:
1. Heat filtered water in a kettle to just before boiling (about 175°F or 80°C). It's important not to overheat the water as it can scorch the delicate tea leaves and alter the flavor.
2. Place the jasmine green tea leaves in the teapot. If you're using a loose leaf teapot with a built-in strainer, that's perfect; otherwise, you may need to use an external strainer when pouring.
3. After pouring the heated water over the tea leaves, infuse the tea for three to four minutes. An individual may alter the steeping period to achieve a more robust or delicate flavor.
4. While the tea is steeping, add 1 teaspoon of lemon juice to each teacup or mug.
5. After steeping, strain the tea as you pour it into the prepared cups with lemon juice.
6. Stir in 1 teaspoon (or to taste) of honey into each cup until dissolved. This not only sweetens the tea but also offers its own natural benefits.
7. Garnish the teacups, if preferred, with recently harvested jasmine flowers to impart an additional aura of sophistication.

BERRY BLAST WHITE TEA INFUSION

Awaken your senses and start the morning with a Berry Blast White Tea Infusion. A delightful concoction blending the subtle, delicate flavors of white tea with the vibrant, tangy notes of fresh berries. It's the perfect morning pick-me-up to kickstart your day with a dose of antioxidants and sweet, fruity undertones.

Equipment: Teapot or saucepan, Tea strainer (optional), Tea cups

Ingredients:
- 2 tablespoons loose leaf white tea
- 1 cup fresh berry mixture, including strawberries, blueberries, and blackberries
- 3 cups filtered water
- 2 teaspoons honey (or to taste)
- fresh mint leaves for garnish (optional)
- ice cubes (for serving cold, optional)

2 servings

5 minutes

7 minutes

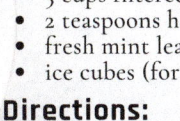

Directions:

1. Remove the water from heat after bringing it to just below simmering. White tea is best steeped with water at 170-185°F (75-85°C) to avoid scalding the delicate leaves.
2. Rinse the mixed berries and gently mash them in a bowl to release their juices and flavors.
3. Place the loose leaf white tea into the teapot or saucepan, add the mashed berries on top, and then pour the hot water over them.
4. Let the tea and berries steep for 5-7 minutes, or to your preferred strength. The longer it steeps, the more pronounced the flavors will be.
5. Strain the tea infusion into tea cups, using a tea strainer if necessary to catch any leaves and berries.
6. Stir in honey to sweeten the infusion to your liking.
7. If serving cold, let the infusion cool for a few minutes then add ice cubes to the cups.
8. Add an extra refreshing minty note by garnishing with a sprig of fresh mint.

Tea Time

ZESTY ORANGE PEKOE PUNCH

Awaken your senses with the Zesty Orange Pekoe Punch, a refreshing and invigorating breakfast tea that combines the robust flavors of Orange Pekoe with the lively essence of fresh citrus. This punch is perfect for jump-starting your day with its zesty brightness and energizing aroma. It is a delightful twist on your morning routine that promises to leave you feeling revitalized and ready to tackle the day ahead.

4 servings   10 minutes   5 minutes

Equipment: Teapot, Citrus Juicer, Measuring cups and spoons, Stirring spoon

Ingredients:
- 4 cups water
- 4 orange pekoe tea bags
- 1/4 cup honey, or to taste
- 1/2 cup fresh orange juice
- 1/4 cup fresh lemon juice
- orange slices and lemon slices, for garnish
- fresh mint leaves, for garnish

Directions:

1. The four glasses of water should be brought to a boil in a large pot or teapot.
2. Once the water is boiling, remove from heat and add the Orange Pekoe tea bags. Steep for 3-5 minutes, depending on how strong you prefer your tea.
3. Whisk in the honey until it is completely dissolved, after removing the tea leaves.
4. While vigorously whisking, incorporate the freshly squeezed orange and lemon juices into the tea.
5. After allowing the tea mixture to reach room temperature, chill it in the refrigerator. If in a rush, you can serve immediately over a generous amount of ice in each cup.
6. Fill glasses to capacity with ice before pouring the Zesty Orange Pekoe Punch over it.
7. Add an additional splash of color and freshness to each glass by garnishing it with segments of orange, lemon, and a sprig of fresh mint.

GINSENG AND GREEN TEA POWER BREW

Begin your day with a cup of Ginseng and Green Tea Power Brew to awaken your senses and inject vitality into your morning routine. Fusing the antioxidant-rich properties of green tea with the revitalizing effects of ginseng, this invigorating concoction is perfect for those seeking an energetic start. Enjoy the subtle earthy tones balanced by the freshness of green tea, creating a harmonious blend that's both fortifying and delicious.

Equipment: Teapot, Measuring spoons, Kettle, Tea cups

Ingredients:
- 2 cups water
- 2 tsp green tea leaves
- 1-2 inch fresh ginseng root, thinly sliced
- 1 tbsp honey (or to taste)
- optional: a few fresh mint leaves

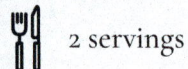

2 servings
5 minutes
10 minutes

Directions:
1. Bring the water to just short of boiling in a kettle to preserve the delicate nature of green tea leaves.
2. Add the thinly sliced ginseng root to your teapot and pour in the hot water. Let it steep for 5 minutes to allow the ginseng to begin releasing its flavor and beneficial properties.
3. Stew the green tea leaves for an additional three minutes in the teapot. Avoid over-steeping, as this can cause bitterness in the flavor of the green tea.
4. Strain the brew into tea cups, ensuring that no tea leaves or ginseng slices are poured into the cups.
5. Incorporate one tablespoon of honey into each cup of tepid tea to enhance the flavor profile of the ginseng and tea while it retains its natural sweetness.
6. Garnish with a few fresh mint leaves in each cup, if desired, for an added refreshing note to your energizing morning beverage.

Zen Sip

INVIGORATING LEMONGRASS MATE

Wake up your morning with the stimulating blend of Invigorating Lemongrass Mate. A perfect concoction for those who love a brisk start. This recipe merges the bold, earthy flavors of yerba mate with the fresh, citrusy notes of lemongrass, creating an energizing and revitalizing beverage that's sure to kickstart your day.

Equipment: Teapot or saucepan, Strainer, Measuring spoons, Measuring cup

Ingredients:
- 2 tbsp dried yerba mate leaves
- 1 tbsp fresh lemongrass, chopped or 1 teabag of lemongrass tea
- 1 tsp honey, or to taste (optional)
- 2 cups water
- lemon slice for garnish (optional)

2 servings   5 minutes   10 minutes

Directions:
1. In a teapot or saucepan, bring 2 cups of water to a soft boil.
2. Reduce heat and add the dried yerba mate leaves and chopped lemongrass.
3. Simmer for 5 minutes, allowing the leaves to infuse their flavor into the water. If you're using a lemongrass tea bag, let it steep for the same amount of time.
4. Take off the heat and strain the tea mixture to remove the leaves and lemongrass pieces.
5. If desired, sweeten the tea with a teaspoon of honey, or to taste.
6. If desired, garnish the Invigorating Lemongrass Mate in serving containers with a lemon slice.

CARDAMOM AND CLOVE MORNING TEA

Wake up to a warm, aromatic cup of Cardamom and Clove Morning Tea. Perfect for invigorating the senses and adding a little spice to your day, this blend not only energizes but also comforts with its harmonious combination of exotic spices. Commence your morning with this robust-flavored tea, complemented by an ideal equilibrium of sweetness and warmth.

Equipment: Teapot, Stove, Measuring Spoons, Strainer

Ingredients:
- 2 cups water
- 2 teaspoons of loose black tea leaves or 2 black tea bags
- 1/4 tsp ground cardamom
- 4 whole cloves
- 1 cinnamon stick
- 2 tsp honey, or to taste
- milk or milk alternative, to taste (optional)

2 servings

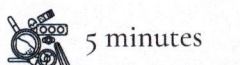

5 minutes

10 minutes

Directions:
1. Put 2 cups of water in a teapot and heat over medium heat until it boils.
2. Once the water is boiling, add the black tea bags or loose tea leaves, ground cardamom, whole cloves, and cinnamon stick.
3. Allow the tea to percolate for approximately 5 minutes to allow the flavors to permeate. If a stronger spice flavor is desired, let it simmer for up to 10 minutes.
4. Strain the tea into cups to eliminate the tea leaves and seasonings after removing the teapot from the heat.
5. Stir in honey to each cup according to your sweetness preference.
6. If desirable, incorporate a small amount of milk or an alternative milk substitute to achieve a creamy consistency and mitigate the intensity of the robust spices.

Tea Delight

POMEGRANATE PANACHE BLACK TEA

This Pomegranate Panache Black Tea infuses the robust, deep flavors of a quality black tea with the tangy, sweet notes of fresh pomegranate. It's an invigorating blend that will wake up your senses and provide a delightful start to any morning. The perfect beverage to kickstart your day with an energizing yet satisfyingly fruity twist.

Equipment: Teapot, Kettle, Measuring Spoon, Strainer, Teacups

Ingredients:
- 2 tbsp loose leaf black tea
- 1 cup fresh pomegranate juice
- 2 cups water
- 1 tbsp honey (or to taste)
- pomegranate arils, for garnish
- fresh mint leaves, for garnish (optional)

2 servings   5 minutes   10 minutes

Directions:
1. In a kettle, bring to a boil two glasses of water to begin..
2. Pour the water that has been brought to a roaring boil over the loose leaf black tea in the teapot. Tea should percolate for three to five minutes, based on personal preference for strength.
3. Pour out the pomegranate juice into a saucepan and heat it over medium heat while the tea steeps, until it is heated but not boiling.
4. Pour out the brewed tea into the heated pomegranate juice after the tea has steeped, filtering the leaves. While stirring, completely dissolve the honey.
5. If desired, briefly reheat the tea and pomegranate mixture on low heat until it reaches your preferred drinking temperature.
6. For a revitalizing touch of green, transfer the Pomegranate Panache Black Tea to individual teacups and adorn with pomegranate arils and a few fresh mint leaves as garnish.

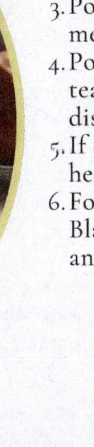

REFRESHING FENNEL AND GREEN TEA BLEND

Awaken your senses with this invigorating tea blend that pairs the grassy notes of green tea with the subtle sweetness and refreshing licorice-like flavor of fennel. Perfect for starting your morning with an energizing yet soothing cup that truly refreshes.

Equipment: Teapot with infuser, Kettle, Measuring spoons

Ingredients:
- 2 teaspoons green tea leaves
- 1 teaspoon fennel seeds, lightly crushed
- 2 cups boiling water
- honey or sweetener of choice (optional)
- lemon wedge for garnish (optional)

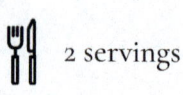

2 servings

5 minutes

5 minutes

Directions:
1. Two glasses of water should be brought to a boil. While the water is heating, add the green tea leaves and lightly crushed fennel seeds to the teapot infuser.
2. Remove the water from the flame when it reaches a rolling boil and allow it to cool for approximately 30 seconds. Green tea is best brewed with water around 80-85°C (175-185°F), not boiling, to avoid bitterness.
3. Pour out the hot water over the green tea and fennel seed mixture in the teapot. Delay steeping the tea for three minutes. Longer steeping time may make the tea bitter.
4. After steeping, carefully remove the infuser from the teapot to prevent further brewing. If you prefer a sweeter cup, add honey or your chosen sweetener to taste.
5. If applicable, incorporate the sweetener gradually to ensure complete dissolution.
6. Pour the tea into cups and if desired, garnish each cup with a lemon wedge.

Sip Slowly

BOLD BREAKFAST PU-ERH

Start your morning with the Bold Breakfast Pu-erh—a robust and earthy tea that is known for its energizing properties. This fermented tea features a deep, rich flavor and an aroma that awakens the senses. Its smooth taste is the perfect foundation for a kick of spice and a hint of citrus, offering a unique twist on traditional breakfast teas.

2 servings   5 minutes   10 minutes

Equipment: Teapot, Kettle, Measuring spoon, Fine mesh strainer

Ingredients:
- 4 tsp loose leaf pu-erh tea
- 2 cups boiling water
- 1 tsp honey, or to taste
- 2 slices of fresh ginger
- 2 strips of orange zest
- 1/4 tsp ground cinnamon
- a pinch of black pepper
- milk or substitute (optional)

Directions:
1. In a kettle, bring to a boil two glasses of water to begin. If you have a temperature-controllable kettle, set it to 212°F (100°C) which is the perfect temperature for Pu-erh.
2. Add the loose leaf Pu-erh tea, ginger slices, orange zest, ground cinnamon, and black pepper into your teapot.
3. When the water in the teapot reaches a roiling boil, pour it over the ingredients..
4. Allow the tea to infuse in a covered teapot for seven to ten minutes. Pu-erh tea is more forgiving than other teas and won't become bitter if steeped longer.
5. While the tea is steeping, warm your serving cups with a bit of hot water to keep your tea warmer for longer once served.
6. After steeping, stir in the honey until it dissolves. Optionally, you can add milk to create a richer and smoother tea.
7. Place the fine mesh strainer over your cups and pour the tea to filter out the tea leaves and other ingredients.
8. Discard the used tea leaves and other solids after straining.

A World of Tea Recipes

Afternoon Teas: Refresh and Revitalize

APRICOT ORCHARD OOLONG

An essence of sunrise captured in a cup, this Apricot Orchard Oolong is an invigorating blend that will energize your morning with its delightful fruitiness and the sophisticated depth of oolong tea. Perfect for those who appreciate a touch of natural sweetness and complex aromas to start their day.

Equipment: Teapot with strainer, Kettle, Measuring spoons, Teacups

Ingredients:

- 2 teaspoons oolong tea leaves
- 2 cups filtered water
- 1-2 fresh apricots, pitted and sliced (or 3 tablespoons apricot preserves if fresh aren't available)
- 1 tablespoon honey or to taste
- optional: fresh mint leaves for garnish

2 servings

5 minutes

7 minutes

Directions:

1. Heat the filtered water in a kettle until it reaches about 185°F (85°C), just below boiling, ideal for brewing oolong tea.
2. Place the Oolong tea leaves in the teapot strainer.
3. Gently pour the heated water over the tea leaves and allow them to steep for 5-7 minutes depending on desired strength. Meanwhile, prepare the apricot slices or if using preserves, set them aside.
4. While the tea is steeping, divide the fresh apricot slices or apricot preserves between the two teacups.
5. Once the tea has steeped, remove the strainer to halt the brewing process.
6. Pour the hot tea over the apricots or preserves in the teacups, allowing them to infuse with the fruit flavors for a moment.
7. Stir in honey to each cup to sweeten the tea according to personal taste preferences.
8. As an additional visual and aromatic touch, garnish with freshly picked mint leaves, if desired.

Enjoy yourself

LAVENDER BREEZE CHAMOMILE INFUSION

Awaken your senses with this tranquil Lavender Breeze Chamomile Infusion. A harmonious blend of calming chamomile and aromatic lavender delivers a soothing aroma and a gentle touch of flavor, perfect for starting your day with tranquility and ease. The delicate floral notes will provide an early morning retreat, setting a serene tone for the day ahead.

2 servings   5 minutes   3 minutes

Equipment: Teapot or French press, Kettle, Measuring spoons

Ingredients:

- 2 cups water
- 2 tbsp dried chamomile flowers
- 1 tsp dried lavender buds
- 1 tsp honey, or to taste
- 1 lemon slice (optional, for garnish)
- fresh lavender sprigs (optional, for garnish)

Directions:

1. In order to commence, heat two glasses of water to just below the boiling point.. You want the water hot enough to steep the herbs but not so hot that it destroys the delicate flavors.
2. Place the dried chamomile flowers and lavender buds into the teapot or French press.
3. Pour the hot water over the chamomile and lavender, making sure that the herbs are fully submerged.
4. Allow the infusion to steep for 5 minutes. This will ensure the flavors are fully extracted while maintaining the soothing properties of the herbs.
5. After 5 minutes, strain the infusion into cups or mugs to remove the herbs. If you used a French press, simply press down the plunger to separate the herbs from the water.
6. Sweeten the infusion with a teaspoon of honey, adjusting to your preference.
7. If desired, garnish each cup with a slice of lemon or a fresh sprig of lavender for an added touch of elegance and flavor.

PEACH PERFECTION WHITE TEA

Start your day with the subtlety of white tea infused with the sweet, sun-ripened charm of peach. This delicate Peach Perfection White Tea combines the gentle, soothing properties of traditional white tea with the vibrant, aromatic flavors of fresh peaches. It's a light, refreshing beverage that's perfect for awakening your senses in the morning and helping you greet the day with a tranquil yet upbeat spirit.

Equipment: Teapot with strainer, Kettle, Measuring spoons, Teacups

Ingredients:

- 4 cups filtered water
- 4 tsp white tea leaves
- 1 large ripe peach, pitted and sliced
- 2 tbsp honey (or to taste)
- fresh mint leaves (for garnish, optional)

4 servings
5 minutes
7 minutes

Directions:

1. Precede boiling by bringing the water to a gentle simmer. White tea is best brewed with water around 175°F to 185°F (80-85°C) to prevent bitterness.
2. Place the white tea leaves into the heatproof teapot.
3. Add the fresh peach slices to the tea leaves. You can muddle them slightly to release more flavor if desired.
4. Pour out the hot water into the teapot over the tea leaves and peach slices, and let steep for 4 to 5 minutes. White tea requires a shorter brewing time compared to black or green teas.
5. As the tea steeps, gradually incorporate honey into the cups, making sure to modify the quantity to your preferred sweetness.
6. After the tea has steeped, strain it into the cups, ensuring the peach slices and leaves are left behind.
7. Stir the tea gently to fully dissolve the honey.

FLORAL SYMPHONY ROSE TEA

Tea Time

Invigorate your morning senses with Floral Symphony Rose Tea, a warming and aromatic blend that harmonizes the delicate notes of rose with robust black tea. Perfect for inspiring a tranquil yet energized start to your day, this tea captures the poetic essence of a blooming garden at dawn.

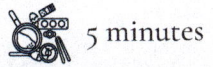

2 servings 5 minutes 5 minutes

Equipment: Teapot, Teacup, Strainer (optional)

Ingredients:

- 2 tsp black tea leaves
- 1 tbsp dried rose petals
- 2 cups boiling water
- 1 tsp honey or to taste
- 1 tbsp rose water (optional for a stronger rose flavor)
- edible rose petals for garnishing (optional)

Directions:

1. Heat your water until it's just boiling.
2. Place the black tea leaves and dried rose petals in the teapot.
3. Pour out the boiling water over the tea leaves and rose petals, ensuring they are fully immersed.
4. Allow the tea to infuse for three to five minutes, depending on your preferred strength. An optional step for rose enthusiasts is to add rose water for an intensified floral experience.
5. Strain the tea into your teacups, discarding the leaves and petals.
6. Sweeten with honey to your preferred taste.
7. If desired, garnish with edible rose petals to enchant your senses further and enhance the floral appeal.

CITRUS HARMONY EARL GREY

The stimulating blend of Citrus Harmony Earl Grey will stimulate your senses. This tea is a twist on the classic Earl Grey, featuring vibrant citrus notes and bold bergamot that dance together to create a symphony of flavor. Perfect for kick-starting your day with energy and zest, this blend is sure to become a morning favorite for the modern tea lover.

Equipment: Teapot or Tea Infuser, Kettle, Measuring spoons, Citrus juicer

4 servings

5 minutes

5 minutes

Ingredients:

- 2 teaspoons loose leaf earl grey tea
- 1 1/2 cups boiling water
- 1/2 teaspoon organic honey (adjust to taste)
- 1 orange, zest, and juice
- 1 lemon, zest, and juice
- fresh mint leaves for garnish (optional)

Directions:

1. Fill a kettle with 1 1/2 pints of boiling water. Once boiling, let it cool for about a minute to reach the ideal temperature for brewing Earl Grey tea (around 208°F or 98°C).
2. Add the loose leaf Earl Grey tea to the teapot or tea infuser.
3. Scrub the orange and lemon with caution, ensuring to exclude the acrid white pith. Add half of the zest to the tea leaves. Save the remaining zest for garnishing.
4. Stir the tea leaves and citrus zest into the heated water and allow to steep for three to four minutes. This will ensure the flavors are well infused without becoming bitter.
5. While the tea is steeping, juice the orange and lemon. If desirable, strain the juice to remove any seeds or pulp.
6. After the infusion or tea leaves have steeped, remove them from the container.
7. Stir in the citrus juice and honey, adjusting the sweetness to your liking.
8. Using the remaining citrus zest and a sprig of fresh mint, garnish the hot tea before transferring it to heated cups.

MINT MEDLEY GREEN TEA

Zen Sip

Kickstart your morning with the invigorating Mint Medley Green Tea—a harmonious blend of energizing green tea and refreshing mint. Ideal for sipping as the world awakens, this beverage is a fragrant reminder to embrace a new day with zest and vitality.

2 servings   5 minutes   5 minutes

Equipment: Teapot, Teacup, Strainer (optional)

Ingredients:

- 2 tbsp loose leaf green tea
- 1/4 cup fresh mint leaves, slightly bruised to release flavor
- 2 cups filtered water
- honey or sweetener of choice, optional

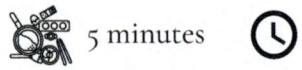

Directions:

1. Bring the filtered water to just before boiling. Approximately 175°F (80°C) is ideal, as too much heat can make the green tea bitter.
2. Fill the teapot halfway with green tea leaves.
3. Sprinkle the fresh mint leaves over the green tea leaves.
4. Pour the hot water into the teapot over the green tea and mint leaves and let it steep for 3 minutes. Adjust the time based on how strong you prefer your tea.
5. While the tea is brewing, contemplate your day ahead and let the rising steam lift your spirits.
6. After steeping, strain the tea into cups or pour over a tea strainer to catch the leaves.
7. Stir in honey or a sweetener of your choice if a hint of sweetness is desired.
8. Gently stir the tea to meld the flavors together.

RASPBERRY HIBISCUS COOLER

Kickstart your morning with the invigorating Raspberry Hibiscus Cooler, a tantalizing blend of sweet raspberries and tangy hibiscus flowers. This vibrant drink is a refreshing alternative to your regular morning brew, offering a burst of fruity flavor along with a gentle caffeine boost.

Equipment: Teapot, Fine Mesh Strainer, Electric Kettle

Ingredients:

- 1/4 cup dried hibiscus flowers
- 1 cup fresh raspberries
- 2 tbsp honey, or to taste
- 4 cups boiling water
- fresh mint leaves (for garnish)
- ice cubes
- optional: 1 tsp green tea leaves (for a caffeine boost)

2 servings

10 minutes

5 minutes

Directions:

1. Start by bringing the water to a full boil in your electric kettle.
2. If you prefer a light caffeine touch, add green tea leaves to the teapot.
3. Pour out the boiling water over the dried hibiscus flowers in the teapot. Include the green tea leaves now if you're using them.
4. Let the tea steep for 5 minutes. If green tea leaves are used, steep for no more than 2-3 minutes to avoid bitterness.
5. While the tea is steeping, muddle the raspberries gently in a bowl to release their juices. Strain the raspberry juice through the fine mesh strainer to remove the seeds. Add honey to the raspberry juice and mix well.
6. Once the tea has steeped, strain it into a large pitcher.
7. Stir in the sweetened raspberry juice into the hibiscus tea until well combined.
8. Fill glasses halfway with ice cubes and top with the Raspberry Hibiscus Cooler. Garnish with fresh mint leaves in each glass.
9. Chill the remainder of the drink in the refrigerator, or serve immediately for a refreshing morning beverage.

MORNING ENERGIZER DARJEELING TEA

Tea Delight

Start your morning off right with Morning Energizer Darjeeling Tea. Known for its bright, aromatic, and refreshing qualities, this exceptional brew hails from the revered tea gardens of Darjeeling, India. It possesses a unique muscatel flavor with a hint of astringency, making it a beloved wake-up call for tea enthusiasts.

4 servings   5 minutes   5 minutes

Equipment: Teapot, Kettle, Measuring spoons, Teacups

Ingredients:

- 4 teaspoons loose leaf darjeeling tea
- 4 cups fresh cold water
- lemon slices (optional)
- honey or sugar to taste (optional)
- fresh mint leaves (optional for garnish)

Directions:

1. Fill your kettle halfway with cold water and bring it to a boil. Darjeeling tea is best brewed with water just under boiling, around 200°F (95 °C).
2. While the water is heating, add 1 teaspoon of loose-leaf Darjeeling tea to your teapot for each cup of tea you're making.
3. Pour out the hot water over the tea leaves in the teapot once it has reached the proper temperature.
4. Allow 3–4 minutes for the tea to steep. Your strength preference will decide the precise time. A shorter steeping time yields a lighter, more mellow cup, while a longer steep allows for a more robust flavor.
5. After steeping, stir the tea gently and then strain it into teacups.
6. If desired, sweeten with honey or sugar and add a lemon slice to complement the natural flavors of the Darjeeling tea.

BERGAMOT BLISS HERBAL TISANE

Begin your morning with Bergamot Bliss Herbal Tisane, a tea blend that combines the citrusy sophistication of bergamot with the subtle spicy notes of ginger and the sweetness of licorice root. This herbal infusion is a perfect energizer to awaken the senses and start the day with a clear mind and revitalized spirit.

Equipment: Teapot, Strainer, Measuring spoons, Kettle

Ingredients:

- 1 tablespoon dried bergamot leaves (or earl grey if pure bergamot leaves are unavailable)
- 1 teaspoon dried ginger pieces
- 1/2 teaspoon licorice root, ground (or small pieces)
- 2 cups freshly boiled water
- optional: honey or lemon slices for serving

2 servings

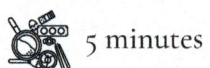

5 minutes

10 minutes

Directions:

1. Begin by boiling the water in your kettle. While the water is boiling, measure and prepare the dried bergamot leaves, dried ginger, and licorice root.
2. Place the dried bergamot leaves, dried ginger pieces, and licorice root into the teapot.
3. When the water is boiling, pour it over the tea blend in the teapot.
4. Cover the teapot with a lid and let the herbal tisane steep for 10 minutes to allow the flavors and properties of the herbs to fully infuse into the water.
5. After steeping, carefully strain the tisane into tea cups to remove the herb pieces.
6. To emphasize the citrus overtones, sweeten with honey or garnish with a slice of lemon.
7. Stir gently before savoring the first rejuvenating sip.

Sip Slowly

CARAMEL WHISPER BLACK TEA

Start your morning with the velvety indulgence of "Caramel Whisper Black Tea". This rich, bold black tea blend is softly kissed by the luxurious notes of buttery caramel, giving it a seductive sweet edge without overindulging. It's a subtle nod to a decadent dessert transformed into a soothing, warm beverage that will gently wake your senses and prepare you for the day ahead.

2 servings   5 minutes   5 minutes

Equipment: Teapot or Saucepan, Measuring Spoons, Teaspoons, Tea Strainer or Infuser, Small Pot for Caramel Sauce

Ingredients:

- 2 cups water
- 2 teaspoons black tea leaves, or 2 black tea bags
- 2 tablespoons caramel sauce (store-bought or homemade)
- 2 teaspoons brown sugar (optional, for extra sweetness)
- milk or cream to taste (optional)

Directions:

1. In a teapot or saucepan, bring 2 cups of water to a rolling simmer to begin.
2. Add the black tea leaves to the water using a tea strainer or infuser. If you're using tea bags, simply drop them into the water.
3. Allow 3-4 minutes for the tea to steep, depending on the strength you desire.
4. While the tea is steeping, if you choose to make your own caramel sauce, gently heat sugar in a small pot over medium heat until it starts to melt and turn brown, being careful not to burn it. Add a touch of cream and stir until a smooth sauce forms, then set aside.
5. Once the tea is steeped, remove the tea leaves or bags.
6. Stir in the caramel sauce until it's fully dissolved. If using, add brown sugar for extra sweetness and stir until dissolved.
7. If desirable, pour the scalding caramel black tea into cups and garnish with a splash of milk or cream. Mildly stir in order to achieve the ideal creamy consistency.
8. If additional sweetness is required, adjust by stirring in a little more caramel sauce or brown sugar until the desired sweetness is achieved.

SUMMER BERRY SANGRIA TEA

Start your morning with a refreshing burst of berries in this Summer Berry Sangria Tea. This invigorating blend of sweet and tangy flavors is perfect for recharging your senses and providing a delightful twist to your typical breakfast tea. Its vibrant hues and uplifting aroma make this tea a beautiful and energizing addition to any morning routine.

Equipment: Large Pitcher, Tea Infuser or Strainer, Saucepan

Ingredients:
- 4 cups water
- 4 black tea bags (or 2 tbsp loose leaf black tea)
- 1/2 cup fresh strawberries, sliced
- 1/2 cup fresh raspberries
- 1/4 cup fresh blueberries
- 1/4 cup fresh blackberries
- 1 orange, sliced into thin rounds
- 1/4 cup honey (or to taste)
- ice cubes (for serving)
- fresh mint leaves (for garnishing)

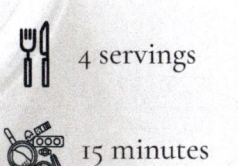

4 servings
15 minutes
5 minutes

Directions:
1. Water that has been brought to a rolling simmer in a saucepan is poured into a heatproof pitcher containing the tea bags or loose leaf tea. Five minutes prior to removing the tea bags or straining the leaves, permit the tea to percolate.
2. While the tea is steeping, add a handful of each type of berry to the pitcher. Squeeze in a few rounds of orange, adding them to the pitcher as well.
3. Once the honey is completely dissolved in the tea, stir it in.
4. Place the pitcher in the refrigerator and allow the tea to cool for about 10 minutes. The tea will also infuse with the flavors of the fruit during this time.
5. Fill glasses with ice cubes and pour the chilled sangria tea over them, making sure each glass gets a generous amount of the berries and a slice or two of the orange.
6. Garnish each glass with fresh mint leaves.

Enjoy yourself

JASMINE JEWEL GREEN TEA

Begin your day with the aromatic embrace of Jasmine Jewel Green Tea. A fragrance to awaken the senses, coupled with a light caffeine boost to start your morning with tranquility and energy. This blend harmoniously combines the floral sweetness of jasmine with the subtle, yet distinct, grassy notes of green tea, creating an invigorating elixir that is both soothing and revitalizing.

2 servings   5 minutes   5 minutes

Equipment: Teapot, Tea strainer or infuser, Kettle

Ingredients:
- 2 teaspoons jasmine green tea leaves
- 16 ounces filtered water
- optional: honey or sweetener of choice, to taste
- optional garnish: jasmine blossoms or a slice of lemon

Directions:
1. Begin by bringing the filtered water to just below boiling (about 175°F to 185°F (80-85°C)). If you do not have a temperature-controlled kettle, allow boiling water to sit for a minute before using it to prevent burning the delicate green tea leaves.
2. Place the jasmine green tea leaves into the tea strainer or infuser, then position it inside the teapot.
3. Once the water is at the correct temperature, pour it over the tea leaves, ensuring they are fully submerged.
4. Steep the tea for 3 minutes. Green tea can become bitter if over-steeped, so keep an eye on the timing.
5. After steeping, carefully remove the tea strainer or infuser from the pot to halt the brewing process.
6. If desired, add honey or another sweetener, and stir gently until fully dissolved.
7. Pour the tea into individual cups, straining if necessary to catch any leaves that might escape the infuser.

GOLDEN CHRYSANTHEMUM BREW

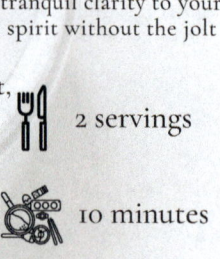

Start your day with a warm cup of Golden Chrysanthemum Brew, an invigorating beverage with vibrant golden hues and a gentle floral sweetness. Traditionally revered in East Asian culture for its health benefits, this blend is believed to awaken the senses and offer a moment of tranquil clarity to your morning routine. Its delicate flavors will energize the spirit without the jolt often associated with caffeine.

Equipment: Teapot or heatproof glass teapot, Kettle, Fine-mesh strainer

Ingredients:
- 1/4 cup dried chrysanthemum flowers (or 2 individual chrysanthemum tea bags)
- 2 cups boiling water
- 2 tsp honey, or to taste
- 2 thin slices fresh ginger (optional)
- lemon zest strips from 1/2 lemon (optional)

2 servings
10 minutes
5 minutes

Directions:
1. Begin by bringing the water to a boil in your kettle. While waiting, rinse the chrysanthemum flowers in cool water if using loose flowers.
2. Place the chrysanthemum flowers or bags in your teapot.
3. Once the water reaches a boil, pour it over the chrysanthemum flowers and add the ginger slices and lemon zest if desired.
4. Cover the teapot and let the brew steep for 5 minutes. The steeping time can be adjusted based on your flavor strength preference.
5. After steeping, carefully strain the tea to remove the flowers and any large pieces of zest or ginger. Be gentle as chrysanthemum petals are quite delicate.
6. Stir in honey to sweeten the brew according to your liking.
7. Pour the fragrant Golden Chrysanthemum Brew into two cups, evenly distributing the liquid.

CHERRY BLOSSOM SENCHA

Tea Time

Experience the dazzling fusion of delicate sencha green tea and the fragrant allure of cherry blossoms with this Cherry Blossom Sencha recipe. Designed to invoke the serene beauty of a cherry blossom spring morning, this tea is an uplifting and rejuvenating way to energize your day.

2 servings
5 minutes
3 minutes

Equipment: Teapot with infuser, Kettle, Teacups

Ingredients:
- 12 oz filtered water
- 2 tsp sencha green tea leaves
- 1 tbsp dried cherry blossoms (sakura), edible grade
- 1 tsp honey or to taste (optional)

Directions:
1. Begin by boiling the filtered water to just before it reaches a rolling boil, around 175°F (80°C). It's important not to overheat as sencha is delicate and can become bitter when steeped in water that's too hot.
2. Place the sencha green tea leaves and dried cherry blossoms into the infuser section of your teapot.
3. Pour out the heated water over the tea leaves and cherry blossoms. Allow 2-3 minutes for the tea to steep. This quick steeping time helps preserve the sencha's natural umami flavors and avoids bitterness.
4. While waiting, you may wish to warm your teacups with some additional hot water, which can be discarded before serving the tea.
5. Once steeped, remove the infuser to prevent over-extraction and pour the infused tea into the warmed teacups.
6. If desired, stir in a teaspoon of honey to each cup for a touch of sweetness that complements the floral notes of the cherry blossoms.

LEMON VERBENA AND THYME TONIC

Begin your morning with a zesty clarity from the Lemon Verbena and Thyme Tonic. This invigorating herbal drink combines the bright, citrusy notes of lemon verbena with the earthy undertones of thyme, creating a perfect balance to awaken the senses. This tonic is not only a stimulating start to the day but also a delightful way to boost your wellness routine.

Equipment: Teapot, Fine-mesh strainer, Teacups

Ingredients:
- 2 cups water
- 2 tbsp fresh lemon verbena leaves
- 1 tbsp fresh thyme sprigs
- 1 tsp honey, or to taste
- fresh lemon slices, for garnish

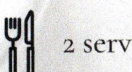

2 servings
10 minutes
5 minutes

Directions:
1. In a teapot or saucepan, bring 2 cups of water to a near boil.
2. Add the fresh lemon verbena leaves and thyme sprigs to the hot water, let them steep for about 5 minutes. For a stronger flavor, allow to steep for a few additional minutes.
3. While the herbs are steeping, prepare your teacups.
4. Once steeped to your liking, strain the liquid to remove the leaves and thyme, pouring the clear tonic into the prepared teacups.
5. Stir in a teaspoon of honey into each cup, adjusting according to your preferred sweetness.
6. Garnish each teacup with a slice of fresh lemon for an extra pop of citrus.

Zen Sip

SPICED ORANGE ROOIBOS

Begin your day with a vibrant Spiced Orange Rooibos tea. This warming beverage combines the naturally sweet, caffeine-free South African rooibos with the zesty brightness of fresh oranges and aromatic spices, creating a perfect morning energizer that's both heartening and fortifying.

2 servings   10 minutes   5 minutes

Equipment: Teapot or saucepan, Strainer, Zester or grater, Knife, Cutting board

Ingredients:
- 4 tsp rooibos tea
- 2 cups boiling water
- 1 medium-sized orange
- 2 tsp honey or to taste
- 2 cinnamon sticks
- 4 cloves
- 1/4 tsp ground nutmeg
- 1/4 tsp ground ginger
- orange slices or zest for garnish (optional)
- cinnamon sticks for garnish (optional)

Directions:
1. Bring two cups of water to a boil.
2. While the water is heating, zest the orange with a zester or grater, avoiding the bitter white pith beneath the orange skin.
3. Slice the orange in half and squeeze the juice from one half into a teapot or heatproof container. Cut the remaining half of the orange into thin slices for garnish (optional).
4. Add the rooibos tea, orange zest, cinnamon sticks, cloves, ground nutmeg, and ground ginger to the teapot or saucepan.
5. Once the water reaches a boil, pour it over the spiced tea mixture and steep for 5 minutes. The heat will activate the spices and release their flavors.
6. After steeping, strain the mixture to remove the solids and pour the infused tea into mugs or glasses.
7. Stir in honey to sweeten to your liking.
8. Garnish each serving with a slice of orange or a sprinkle of orange zest and a cinnamon stick for a sophisticated touch.

APPLE CINNAMON MORNING ENERGIZER

Wake up to a warm, inviting blend of apple and cinnamon that perfectly complements your morning routine. This tea is not only tantalizing in flavor but also offers a gentle energy boost to start your day right. Its comforting aroma and the combination of sweet fruit with a hint of spice are sure to awaken your senses.

Equipment: Teapot or saucepan, Fine mesh strainer, Measuring spoons

Ingredients:

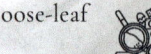

- 4 cups water
- 4 black tea bags (or 2 tablespoons loose-leaf black tea)
- 1 medium apple, cored and sliced
- 2 cinnamon sticks
- 2 tablespoons honey or to taste
- ½ teaspoon vanilla extract
- optional: ¼ cup milk or milk alternative

4 servings
10 minutes
10 minutes

Directions:

1. In a teapot or saucepan, bring water to a gentle boil.
2. Add the black tea bags or loose-leaf tea and let steep for 3-5 minutes, depending on desired strength.
3. Add the sliced apple and cinnamon sticks to the pot and continue to simmer for an additional 5 minutes to infuse the flavors.
4. After removing from heat, thoroughly combine the honey and vanilla extract with a stir. For a creamy twist, you can also add milk or a milk alternative to taste.
5. Pour out the tea through a fine mesh strainer into individual cups to remove the solids.
6. If you used tea bags and want to include the apple slices in the serving, you can divide them among the cups for added texture and flavor.

Tea Delight

GINGER PEACH TEA SPARKLER

Start your day with a bubbly twist on traditional tea. This Ginger Peach Tea Sparkler uses the natural sweetness of peaches and the punch of ginger to create an invigorating morning drink. It's the perfect beverage to awaken the senses and provide a sparkling kick to your morning routine.

4 servings
20 minutes
0 minutes

Equipment: Electric kettle, Pitcher, Spoon, Serving glasses

Ingredients:

- 4 cups water
- 4 bags black tea or 4 teaspoons loose black tea
- 1-inch piece fresh ginger, thinly sliced
- 1 ripe peach, pitted and sliced
- 2 tablespoons honey, or to taste
- 1 teaspoon fresh lemon juice
- 1 cup sparkling water, chilled
- ice cubes
- mint leaves for garnish (optional)

Directions:

1. Heat the water in an electric kettle or on the stovetop until just before it reaches a boil.
2. If using tea bags, place them into the pitcher. If using loose tea, place it in an infuser or directly in the pitcher to be strained out later.
3. Add the sliced ginger and peach slices to the pitcher with the tea.
4. Pour out the hot water over the tea bags, ginger, and peaches. Allow it to steep for 3-5 minutes for a strong brew.
5. Remove the tea bags or strain out the loose tea along with the ginger slices. Allow the tea to cool to room temperature before serving.
6. Honey is thoroughly dissolved in lemon juice and honey; combine with the honey.
7. Place the pitcher in the refrigerator to chill for about 10-15 minutes.
8. When ready to serve, fill serving glasses with ice cubes.
9. Pour the chilled tea over the ice, leaving about ¼ of the glass empty.
10. Top each glass with sparkling water and gently stir to combine.
11. Garnish with a slice of peach and a sprig of mint if desired.

VANILLA ORCHID OOLONG

Start your day with the aromatic embrace of Vanilla Orchid Oolong - a fusion of robust oolong tea laced with gentle whispers of vanilla, creating a cup that is as invigorating as it is comforting. This tea blend provides a perfect balance of energy and tranquility to awaken the senses and prepare you for the morning ahead.

Equipment: Teapot with infuser, Kettle, Measuring spoons

Ingredients:

- 2 teaspoons oolong tea leaves
- 1 vanilla bean pod, or 1 tablespoon pure vanilla extract
- 1 teaspoon honey or preferred sweetener (optional)
- 2 cups freshly boiled water
- edible orchid petals for garnish (optional)

2 servings

5 minutes

7 minutes

Directions:

1. Begin by boiling fresh water to 195°F (90°C) – the ideal temperature to brew oolong tea without scalding the leaves.
2. While the water is boiling, split the vanilla bean pod in half lengthwise and scrape out the seeds using the back of a knife. If using vanilla extract, measure out the tablespoon and set aside.
3. Place the oolong tea leaves into the teapot infuser.
4. Add the vanilla seeds or vanilla extract over the oolong tea leaves in the infuser. If you prefer a sweeter taste, add the honey or sweetener at this step.
5. Once the water reaches the correct temperature, pour it over the tea leaves and vanilla in the infuser. Ensure that the leaves are completely submerged to extract the full flavor.
6. Allow 5 to 7 minutes for the tea to steep, depending on how strong you want your tea. Vanilla Orchid Oolong is best enjoyed at a medium brew to appreciate the taste profile of both tea and vanilla.
7. Remove the infuser from the teapot to prevent the tea from becoming bitter due to over-steeping.
8. Stir the tea gently to ensure the vanilla is well dispersed throughout the brew.

MOROCCAN MINT AND LICORICE TEA

Sip Slowly

Experience the dazzling fusion of delicate sencha green tea and the fragrant allure of cherry blossoms with this Cherry Blossom Sencha recipe. Designed to invoke the serene beauty of a cherry blossom spring morning, this tea is an uplifting and rejuvenating way to energize your day.

4 servings   5 minutes   15 minutes

Equipment: Teapot or saucepan, Strainer, Teacups

Ingredients:

- 4 cups water
- 2 tbsp dried spearmint leaves or green tea leaves
- 1 tbsp licorice root, chopped or in powder form
- 1-2 tbsp honey or to taste (optional, for sweetness)
- fresh mint sprigs for garnish (optional)

Directions:

1. Begin by bringing the water to a boil in your teapot or saucepan.
2. Add the dried spearmint leaves or green tea leaves and licorice root to the boiling water. If you prefer a stronger licorice flavor, lean towards the higher measurement; if subtlety is your preference, use the smaller suggested amount.
3. Reduce the heat to low and let the tea to simmer for 10-15 minutes, depending on how strong you want your tea.
4. Turn off the heat and allow the tea to steep for an additional 3-5 minutes.
5. Remove the leaves and licorice root from the tea. Serve the tea into individual cups.
6. Sweeten with honey to your taste, if desired.
7. If you want to boost the presentation and add a bit of minty freshness, garnish each cup with a sprig of fresh mint.

A World of Tea Recipes

Evening Teas: Unwind and Relax

MOONLIGHT CHAMOMILE DREAM

This tranquil Moonlight Chamomile Dream is a gentle lullaby in a cup, perfect for relaxing the mind and soothing the soul after a long day. A delicate blend of chamomile, lavender, and a hint of mint, it's designed to ease you into a restful evening and sweet slumber under the stars.

Equipment: Teapot with infuser, Kettle, Measuring spoons

Ingredients:
- 2 tablespoons dried chamomile flowers
- 1 teaspoon lavender buds dried
- 1 tablespoon fresh mint leaves, or one teaspoon dried mint
- 2 cups boiling water
- 1 teaspoon honey, or to taste (optional)
- lemon slices, for garnish (optional)

2 servings

5 minutes

10 minutes

Directions:
1. Begin by boiling the 2 cups of water in your kettle. Once boiled, let it sit for a minute to slightly cool – boiling water can scorch the herbs and affect their delicate flavors.
2. Place the dried chamomile flowers and lavender buds into the teapot infuser. If using fresh mint leaves, give them a gentle crush with your fingers to release their oils, and then add them to the infuser. If you're using dried mint, simply add it to the mix.
3. Pour the heated water gradually over the chamomile, lavender, and mint infuser. Allow 5–7 minutes for the tea to steep. The precise duration will be determined by your taste choice for the intensity of the herbal tea.
4. After steeping, carefully remove the infuser from the teapot to avoid the tea becoming bitter from over-steeping.
5. If you'd like a touch of sweetness, stir in a teaspoon of honey to each cup until it dissolves.
6. Pour the Moonlight Chamomile Dream into cups and, if desired, add a thin slice of lemon for an extra bit of calming citrus aroma.

Enjoy yourself

TWILIGHT LAVENDER SOOTHE

Delve into the serene embrace of the evening with Twilight Lavender Soothe, a tranquil herbal infusion designed to calm and comfort before nightfall. This tea blends the soft floral notes of lavender with the gentle warmth of chamomile to create a peaceful potion perfect for easing into a restful night's sleep.

4 servings   5 minutes   10 minutes

Equipment: Teapot or Saucepan, Strainer, Teacups

Ingredients:
- 2 cups water
- 1 tablespoon dried lavender flowers
- 1 tablespoon dried chamomile flowers
- 1 teaspoon honey, or to taste
- a slice of lemon, optional
- fresh lavender sprigs, for garnish

Directions:
1. Begin by boiling the water in your teapot or saucepan.
2. When the water reaches a rolling boil, remove it from the heat and carefully whisk in the dried lavender and chamomile flowers.
3. Cover and let the herbs steep for 5-7 minutes, depending on how strong you prefer your tea.
4. While the tea is steeping, prepare your teacups or mugs.
5. After steeping, strain the tea into the teacups to remove the herb solids.
6. Stir in the honey until completely dissolved, adding more if required.
7. If you enjoy a citrus note in your tea, you may add a thin slice of lemon to each cup.
8. Garnish each cup with a fresh sprig of lavender to enhance the aromatics and present a beautiful visual.

STARLIGHT MINT MELODY

The Starlight Mint Melody is a soothing, caffeine-free herbal concoction perfect for unwinding after a busy day. The refreshing blend of peppermint and chamomile is accented with a hint of honey and the warmth of vanilla, creating a drink that feels like a gentle lullaby for your senses. A touch of lavender lends a floral note, weaving a comforting aroma that prepares you for a restful evening.

Equipment: Teapot, Strainer, Teaspoons, Kettle

Ingredients:

- 1 tablespoon dried peppermint leaves
- 1 tablespoon dried chamomile flowers
- 1/2 teaspoon dried lavender flowers
- 2 cups boiling water
- 1 tablespoon honey (or to taste)
- 1/4 teaspoon vanilla extract

2 servings
10 minutes
5 minutes

Directions:

1. Warm your teapot by rinsing it with hot water. Once warmed, discard the water.
2. Combine the dried peppermint, chamomile, and lavender flowers in the teapot.
3. Pour out two cups of boiling water over the herbal mixture. Stir gently to ensure all herbs are saturated.
4. While covered and steeped for five minutes, the herbs' flavors and properties will permeate the water.
5. While the tea is steeping, stir in the honey and vanilla extract until well combined.
6. After steeping, strain the tea into two cups, ensuring all the herbals are removed.
7. Give each cup a gentle stir to evenly distribute the honey and vanilla.

Tea Time

EVENING ROSE HIP SERENADE

Unwind with the gentle caress of Evening Rose Hip Serenade, a soothing blend perfect for late-night tranquil moments. This heartwarming infusion brings together rose hips' sweet-tart essence and chamomile's calming whispers. With a hint of lavender and honey, each sip is like a serene lullaby that ushers in restful slumber.

2 servings   5 minutes   15 minutes

Equipment: Teapot or saucepan, Strainer, Measuring spoons

Ingredients:

- 4 teaspoons dried rose hips
- 2 teaspoons dried chamomile flowers
- 1 teaspoon dried lavender
- 2 cups boiling water
- 2 teaspoons honey, or to taste
- lemon slices (optional for garnish)
- fresh rose petals (optional for an extra touch of elegance)

Directions:

1. Place the dried rose hips, chamomile flowers, and lavender into the teapot or saucepan.
2. Pour the boiling water over the dried botanicals and cover the teapot or saucepan with a lid. Steep the tea for 15 minutes to fully extract the flavors and beneficial properties of the herbs.
3. After steeping, strain the mixture to remove the solids and pour the liquid into two teacups. Make sure the tea is clear of any small pieces.
4. Stir in a teaspoon of honey into each cup to add natural sweetness and complement the floral notes.
5. If desired, garnish each cup with a lemon slice or throw in a couple of fresh rose petals for a visually appealing and aromatic experience.

CELESTIAL LEMON BALM CALM

Experience a night of peaceful slumber with a cup of Celestial Lemon Balm Calm. This serene infusion combines the soothing properties of lemon balm with the delicate floral notes of chamomile and a hint of lavender. Ideal for unwinding after a long day, its soft, soothing flavors are like a gentle embrace for your senses, guiding you to a state of tranquil relaxation.

Equipment: Teapot or saucepan, Strainer, Teacups

Ingredients:

- 2 cups water
- 2 tablespoons fresh lemon balm leaves, or 2 tsp dried leaves
- 1 tablespoons chamomile flowers
- 1 teaspoon lavender flowers
- 1 teaspoon honey, or to taste
- lemon slices (optional), for garnish

2 servings

10 minutes

10 minutes

Directions:

1. Bring the water to a gentle boil in your teapot or saucepan.
2. Reduce the heat and add the lemon balm leaves, chamomile, and lavender flowers to the hot water.
3. Simmer the herbal mixture on low heat for about 5 minutes.
4. Remove from heat and let it steep, covered, for an additional 5 minutes to enhance the flavors and beneficial properties.
5. Strain the mixture into teacups, pressing on the leaves and flowers to extract all the essences.
6. Stir in honey to sweeten the tea to your taste preference.
7. Garnish with a thin slice of lemon if desired.

Zen Sip

DECAF CEYLON SOLACE

Decaf Ceylon Solace is a tranquil blend perfect for evening relaxation. The mellow yet rich taste of decaffeinated Ceylon tea provides a smooth base for the calming flavors of lavender and vanilla, creating a quiet oasis for your senses.

2 servings   5 minutes   15 minutes

Equipment: Teapot, Measuring Spoons, Tea Cups

Ingredients:

- 2 teaspoons decaffeinated ceylon tea leaves
- 2 cups boiling water
- 1/2 teaspoon dried lavender flowers
- 1 teaspoon vanilla extract
- honey or sweetener of choice to taste
- milk or milk alternative (optional), for serving

Directions:

1. Warm your teapot by filling it with hot water, then discard the water.
2. Place the decaffeinated Ceylon tea leaves and dried lavender flowers into the teapot.
3. Two glasses of boiling water should be poured over the lavender and tea leaves. Four to five minutes, or until the desired strength is reached.
4. Once the tea has reached the preferred strength, strain the tea leaves and lavender flowers, and pour the hot infused tea into tea cups.
5. Stir in the vanilla extract, adding a serene note to your evening cup.
6. To taste, moisten with honey or your preferred sweetener.
7. If preferred, a creamy smoothness can be achieved by adding a dash of milk or a milk substitute to the tea.

NIGHTFALL VALERIAN WHISPER

This enchanting tea blend, the Nightfall Valerian Whisper, is a soothing elixir designed to ease you into a peaceful evening. This tea is infused with the calming qualities of valerian root, which is known for its sleep-promoting benefits, and is complemented by the gentle sweetness of honey and the soothing warmth of chamomile flowers, creating a wonderful nightcap to lull you to sleep.

Equipment: Teapot, Strainer, Teacups

Ingredients:

- 1 ½ teaspoon dried valerian root
- 2 teaspoons dried chamomile flowers
- 1 tablespoon honey (or to taste)
- 2 cups water
- a few sprigs of fresh mint (for garnish)
- ½ teaspoon lavender flowers (optional for an added calming effect)
- lemon slice (for an optional citrusy note)

2 servings
5 minutes
10 minutes

Directions:

1. In a pot or kettle, bring two glasses of water to a gently boiling temperature.
2. Add the dried valerian root to the teapot and pour the hot water over it. Allow it to steep for 5 minutes. Valerian root has a strong earthy taste, which will form the base of the tea's tranquil profile.
3. Add the dried chamomile flowers, and the optional lavender flowers, to the teapot. Steep for another 5 minutes. Chamomile infuses the blend with a soft floral flavor, a traditional ingredient used to reduce stress and promote relaxation.
4. While the tea is steeping, prepare the teacups by placing a teaspoon of honey in each. The honey acts as a natural sweetener to balance the potent flavor of the valerian root.
5. After the tea has steeped, strain it into the teacups, dissolving the honey. Stir gently to mix the honey evenly throughout the tea.
6. If you opt for a touch of lemon, gently squeeze a slice into each cup to add a zesty dimension to the tea's flavor profile.
7. Garnish each cup with a sprig of fresh mint, which adds a refreshing coolness to each sip and further enhances the tea's ability to soothe and relax the senses.

Tea Delight

SUNDOWN SPICED VANILLA

As the sun dips below the horizon, embrace the tranquil serenity of a soothing 'Sundown Spiced Vanilla' tea. This aromatic beverage combines the warm, comforting flavors of vanilla and spices, perfect for unwinding after a long day. Its gentle sweetness and spicy undertones are designed to calm your mind and prepare you for a peaceful evening.

2 servings   5 minutes   10 minutes

Equipment: Teapot or saucepan, Measuring spoons, Strainer, Heatproof mugs

Ingredients:

- 2 cups water
- 2 whole black tea bags or 2 teaspoons loose black tea
- 1 cinnamon stick
- 1/4 teaspoon ground nutmeg
- 2 whole cloves
- 1 star anise
- 1 vanilla pod, split lengthwise (or 1 teaspoon pure vanilla extract)
- 2 teaspoons honey, or to taste
- optional: almond milk or milk of choice for serving

Directions:

1. Pour the water into a teapot or saucepan and bring it to a gentle simmer over medium heat.
2. Once the water is simmering, add the black tea, cinnamon stick, ground nutmeg, cloves, and star anise. If you're using a vanilla pod, scrape out the seeds with the back of a knife, add both the seeds and the pod to the pot; if using vanilla extract, hold off on adding it until later.
3. Reduce the heat and let the tea mixture simmer for around 5-7 minutes, allowing the spices to infuse their flavors into the water.
4. Remove from heat. If you used a vanilla pod, remove and discard the pod and any large spice pieces with a strainer; if using vanilla extract, stir it in now.
5. Add honey to the tea for sweetness and stir until fully dissolved. If you prefer a creamier version of the tea, stir in a splash of warm almond milk or milk of choice.
6. Pour the spiced vanilla tea into heatproof mugs through a strainer to catch any loose tea or remaining spices.

DUSK DELIGHT PASSIONFLOWER

Designed to ease you into a peaceful evening, Dusk Delight Passionflower is a soothing herbal infusion blending the calming properties of passionflower with fragrant herbs. Perfect for sipping as the sky transitions into night, this tea is your companion for relaxation and reflection.

Equipment: Teapot, Strainer, Kettle, Teacup

Ingredients:
- 2 tablespoons dried passionflower
- 2 teaspoons chamomile flowers
- 1 teaspoon lavender buds
- 1/2 teaspoon lemon balm
- 2 cups filtered water
- honey or stevia to taste (optional)
- lemon slices for garnish (optional)

2 servings
10 minutes
5 minutes

Directions:
1. Fill the kettle with 2 cups of filtered water and bring to a boil. Reduce heat and allow water to stop boiling for a minute or two to slightly cool, achieving the optimal temperature for steeping the herbs without losing their delicate flavors.
2. While the water is heating, add the dried passionflower, chamomile flowers, lavender buds, and lemon balm into the teapot.
3. Pour the hot water into the teapot over the herbs and let steep for 5 minutes. This long steeping time allows the full flavor and calming properties of the herbs to infuse into the water.
4. Place the strainer over the teacup and carefully pour the brewed tea to filter out the herbs.
5. If desired, sweeten the tea with honey or stevia to taste and add a slice of lemon for a hint of citrus brightness.

Sip Slowly

MILKY WAY WARM CINNAMON INFUSION

Succumb to the celestial comfort of the Milky Way Warm Cinnamon Infusion. This calming, nightly brew is a perfect companion to unwind after a long day, with its soothing blend of creamy milk, aromatic cinnamon, and subtle sweetness inviting complete relaxation and restful contemplation under a starlit sky.

2 servings   5 minutes   10 minutes

Equipment: Small saucepan, Fine mesh strainer, Measuring cups and spoons

Ingredients:
- 2 cups whole milk or almond milk for a dairy-free option
- 2 cinnamon sticks
- 2 tablespoons loose leaf black tea or 2 black tea bags
- 1 tablespoon honey or to taste
- 1/2 teaspoon pure vanilla extract
- pinch of ground nutmeg
- star anise for garnish (optional)

Directions:
1. To preserve the milk's flavor and avert scalding, heat it gently over medium heat until it begins to steam in a small saucepan. Prevent the milk from boiling to ensure safety.
2. Add the cinnamon sticks to the milk, allowing them to infuse their warm, spicy flavor for about 3-4 minutes.
3. Continue to percolate for 5 minutes, stirring in the black tea, before reducing the heat to low. This will facilitate the fusion of the tea's opulent flavor with the milk.
4. Remove from heat and stir in the honey and vanilla extract, ensuring the honey dissolves thoroughly for a touch of natural sweetness.
5. Let the infusion stand for a minute, then strain the warm beverage into two large mugs, removing the cinnamon sticks and tea leaves or bags.
6. Finish each cup with a light dusting of ground nutmeg and, if desired, a star anise placed on top for an extra hint of licorice-like depth and a visually pleasing touch.

TRANQUIL TULSI AND ORANGE

Tranquil Tulsi and Orange is an enchanting elixir perfect for winding down after a busy day. The herbaceous calm of tulsi, also known as holy basil, pairs harmoniously with the cheerful citrus notes of orange, creating a soothing, aromatic experience that invites relaxation and serenity. A hint of chamomile complements this blend, enhancing its natural ability to ease the mind and pave the way for a peaceful evening.

Equipment: Teapot or saucepan, Strainer, Measuring spoons, Citrus juicer

Ingredients:
- 1 tablespoon dried tulsi leaves (holy basil)
- 1 orange, zest and juice
- 1 teaspoon dried chamomile flowers
- 2 cups water
- 1 tablespoon honey, or to taste (optional)
- fresh orange slices for garnish (optional)

2 servings
5 minutes
15 minutes

Directions:
1. Two glasses of water should be brought to a boil in a teapot or medium saucepan.
2. While the water is heating, zest the orange, being careful to avoid the pith for the best flavor. If you are using a fresh orange, juice it after zesting.
3. Once the water reaches a boil, add the tulsi leaves, orange zest, and chamomile flowers into the pot.
4. By gradually decreasing the heat and maintaining a simmer for a duration of 9 to 15 minutes, a robust herbal tea can be produced through the thorough infusion of flavors.
5. After simmering, remove from heat and strain the tea into two cups, pressing the solids to extract maximum flavor.
6. Add the freshly squeezed orange juice and honey to taste.
7. Serve each cup garnished with a slice of orange, if desired.

Enjoy yourself

RESTFUL ROOIBOS RETREAT

Embrace the calming embrace of Restful Rooibos Retreat, a soothing herbal concoction designed to ease you into a state of deep relaxation. This naturally caffeine-free brew combines the smooth sweetness of rooibos with the tranquil notes of lavender and the comforting warmth of vanilla. Perfect for unwinding after a long day, this blend will become an essential part of your evening wind-down ritual.

2 servings   10 minutes   10 minutes

Equipment: Teapot or Saucepan, Fine Mesh Strainer, Tea Cups

Ingredients:
- 2 tablespoons organic rooibos tea
- 2 cups filtered water
- 1 teaspoon dried lavender flowers
- 1 cinnamon stick
- 1 divided and scraped vanilla pod (or 1 teaspoon pure vanilla extract)
- 1 tablespoon honey (or to taste)
- optional: fresh mint leaves for garnish

Directions:
1. Bring the filtered water to a simmer in a teapot or a small saucepan.
2. Once the water is simmering, add the rooibos tea and dried lavender flowers. If using a vanilla pod, add the pod and scraped seeds to the pot. If using vanilla extract, it will be added later.
3. Cover the container and allow the tea to infuse for 7 to 8 minutes while the heat is reduced. As time passes, the infusion will intensify the floral and vanilla undertones.
4. Remove the tea from the heat once it has steeped. Stir in vanilla extract at this time, if substituting it for a pod.
5. By transferring the mixture to tea glasses via a fine mesh strainer, eliminate any remaining vanilla pods, lavender, and tea leaves.
6. Sweeten the tea with honey, adjusting the amount according to your taste.
7. Stir gently to combine all the flavors.

SERENE SAGE AND HONEY HUSH

A gentle elixir to calm the mind and soothe the spirit, Serene Sage and Honey Hush is a perfect companion for unwinding after a long day. This gracefully simple infusion pairs the earthy tones of sage with the sweet comfort of honey, culminating in a warm, aromatic beverage to help you relax and prepare for a peaceful evening.

Equipment: Teapot or saucepan, Strainer, Teacups

Ingredients:
- 2 cups water
- 1 tablespoon dried sage leaves
- 2 teaspoos honey, or to taste
- 1/4 teaspoon lemon juice
- optional: a few fresh sage leaves (for garnish)

2 servings
5 minutes
10 minutes

Directions:
1. Bring the water to a near boil in a teapot or saucepan. If you're using a teapot with an infuser, you can add the dried sage leaves directly to the infuser. Otherwise, you can add them to the pot and strain them out later.
2. Add the dried sage to the hot water and steep for about 5 minutes. Sage has a strong flavor, so adjust the steeping time according to your taste preference – less time for a milder tea or longer for a more robust flavor.
3. Strain the sage leaves from the water if they weren't in an infuser. Transfer the tea into two teacups.
4. Stir a teaspoon of honey into each cup, adjusting the amount to your liking. Add a couple of drops of lemon juice to each cup for a subtle tanginess that complements the sage.
5. If desired, garnish each cup with a fresh sage leaf before serving to enhance the aroma and visual appeal.

Tea Time

AFTER-DINNER ANISE COMFORT

Unwind after your evening meal with the sweetly aromatic "After-Dinner Anise Comfort" tea. This soothing blend combines the digestive properties of anise with the subtle warmth of ginger and a touch of honey for sweetness. Its licorice-like flavor is perfect for settling the stomach and calming the mind before bedtime.

2 servings   5 minutes   10 minutes

Equipment: Teapot, Strainer, Teacups

Ingredients:
- 2 cups water
- 2 teaspoon whole anise seeds
- 1/2 teaspoon grated ginger
- 1 cinnamon stick
- 2 teaspoons honey, or to taste
- 2 bags of rooibos or chamomile tea
- a squeeze of lemon juice (optional)

Directions:
1. Bring water to a boil in the teapot.
2. Add the whole anise seeds and cinnamon stick to the boiling water, then reduce the heat and simmer for 5 minutes to infuse the flavors.
3. Add grated ginger to the pot and continue to simmer for another 2-3 minutes for a spicy warmth.
4. Remove from heat and add the rooibos or chamomile tea bags, allowing them to steep for 5 minutes. Rooibos is naturally caffeine-free and chamomile is known for its calming properties, either choice is excellent for an evening wind-down.
5. Remove the tea bags, strain out the anise seeds, cinnamon stick, and ginger.
6. Stir in honey until it dissolves and add a squeeze of lemon juice if desired for a hint of citrus.
7. Pour the tea into cups, making sure it's well-strained and clear.

PEACEFUL PEPPERMINT AND LICORICE

This Peaceful Peppermint and Licorice tea blend is the perfect way to end your day. With a soothing combination of minty freshness and sweet, earthy licorice, this caffeine-free herbal infusion promotes relaxation and tranquility. The peppermint helps calm the body, while licorice is known for its naturally sweet, comforting properties, making it an ideal choice for unwinding before bedtime.

Equipment: Medium saucepan, Strainer or tea infuser, Teapot or teacups

Ingredients:
- 2 cups water
- 1 tablespoon dried peppermint leaves
- 1 teaspoon licorice root, chopped or in powder form
- 1 teaspoon honey or maple syrup (optional)
- a few fresh peppermint leaves for garnish (optional)

2 servings

5 minutes

10 minutes

Directions:
1. Bring the water to a simmer in a medium saucepan.
2. Stir together the desiccated peppermint leaves and licorice root with the water. Ten minutes later, reduce the heat to low, cover, and allow the mélange to simmer. As the simmer time increases, so do the intensity of the flavors.
3. Remove from heat. If you've used chopped licorice root, strain the tea mixture to remove the pieces or use a tea infuser to avoid them in the first place.
4. Pour the hot infusion into teacups or a teapot, using a strainer if necessary.
5. If desired, stir in a teaspoon of honey or maple syrup to add a natural sweetness to the tea.
6. Garnish with fresh peppermint leaves for a refreshing aroma and a touch of elegance.

Zen Sip

SLUMBERING LOTUS STEEP

Slip into a serene state before bedtime with the Slumbering Lotus Steep, an exquisite blend designed to calm the mind and ease into a restful night. The lotus flower, renowned for its soothing properties, takes center stage in this tranquil concoction. Paired with the gentle notes of chamomile and the sweetness of honey, this tea ensures a peaceful transition to dreamland.

2 servings   5 minutes   5 minutes

Equipment: Teapot or saucepan, Strainer, Measuring spoons, Teacups

Ingredients:
- 2 teaspoons dried lotus flowers
- 2 teaspoons chamomile flowers
- 1 teaspoon lavender buds
- 2 cups filtered water
- 2 teaspoons honey, or to taste
- lemon wedge, optional for a touch of citrus

Directions:
1. Bring the filtered water to a gentle boil in a teapot or saucepan.
2. Once the water reaches the boiling point, reduce the heat and add the dried lotus flowers, chamomile flowers, and lavender buds.
3. Cover and let the herbs steep for 5 minutes, allowing their flavors and soothing properties to infuse the water.
4. After steeping, strain the mixture into teacups, ensuring that the herb residues are removed.
5. Stir in a teaspoon of honey into each cup or adjust to your preferred sweetness.
6. If desired, squeeze a small wedge of lemon into each cup for a subtle, refreshing citrus twist.

QUIET TIME TANGERINE BLEND

This Quiet Time Tangerine Blend is the perfect way to settle down after a long day. The sweet, citrusy notes of tangerine blend harmoniously with the soothing effects of chamomile and the subtle warmth of cinnamon. A hint of honey adds a touch of natural sweetness, making this tea an ideal companion for quiet evenings or moments of reflection.

Equipment: Teapot or saucepan, Fine mesh strainer, Teacups

Ingredients:

- 4 cups water
- 2 tangerine peel strips, about 3 inches each
- 2 tablespoons loose leaf chamomile tea, or 2 chamomile tea bags
- 1 cinnamon stick
- 1 tablespoons honey or to taste
- optional: a few sprigs of fresh mint for garnish

2 servings
5 minutes
10 minutes

Directions:

1. Bring water to a near boil in a teapot or saucepan.
2. Add the tangerine peel strips and let them steep for 2-3 minutes.
3. Place loose leaf chamomile tea in a tea infuser or directly add chamomile tea bags to the pot. Add the cinnamon stick.
4. Lower the heat and allow the tea blend to simmer gently for another 5-7 minutes.
5. Remove from heat and carefully strain the tea into cups, removing the tangerine peels, cinnamon stick, and tea bags.
6. Stir in a tablespoon of honey, adjusting according to your preferred sweetness.
7. If desired, garnish each cup with a fresh sprig of mint for a refreshing touch.

Tea Delight

COZY CLOVE AND COCOA TISANE

This warming tisane is a hug in a mug, perfect for unwinding in the evening. Aromatic cloves and soothing cocoa blend together to create a comforting, caffeine-free beverage to ease into the night. With a hint of sweetness and a touch of spice, the Cozy Clove and Cocoa Tisane is your ideal companion for relaxation and reflection.

2 servings
10 minutes
15 minutes

Equipment: Teapot or saucepan, Strainer, Measuring spoons, Teacups

Ingredients:

- 2 cups water
- 1 tablespoon dried clove buds
- 2 tablespoons cocoa nibs
- 1 stick cinnamon
- 1 tablespoon honey, or to taste
- 1/4 teaspoon vanilla extract
- an optional dash of milk or an alternative milk substitute
- orange peel twist, for garnish (optional)

Directions:

1. Bring the water to a gentle boil in a teapot or saucepan.
2. Once boiling, add the dried clove buds, cocoa nibs, and cinnamon stick. Ten to fifteen minutes at a simmer over reduced heat will allow the flavors to fully infuse.
3. After turning off the heat, combine honey and vanilla extract. Modify the degree of flavor to suit personal preference.
4. Strain the tisane through a tea strainer or fine mesh sieve into cups, making sure to catch all the clove buds and cocoa nibs.
5. To impart a creamy consistency to your tisane, you may, if desired, add a dash of milk or an alternative milk sweetener.
6. An orange peel spiral serves as a garnish, contributing a zesty citrus flavor.

SLEEPY THYME EMBRACE

This soothing tea blend is the perfect elixir for relaxation before bedtime. The Sleepy Thyme Embrace is a delicate mixture of calming chamomile, fragrant thyme, and subtle hints of lavender and mint. It is designed to ease your mind and prepare you for a restful night's sleep. The gentle warmth and aromatic bouquet of this tea provide a relaxing experience for the senses.

Equipment: Teapot, Strainer, Kettle, Measuring Spoons

Ingredients:
- 2 cups filtered water
- 2 teaspoons dried chamomile flowers
- 1 teaspoon fresh thyme leaves
- 1 teaspoon dried lavender flowers
- 1 teaspoon honey (optional)
- 2 fresh mint leaves (for garnish)

2 servings
10 minutes
5 minutes

Directions:
1. In a kettle, bring the filtered water to a gentle simmer..
2. While waiting for the water to boil, place the dried chamomile flowers, thyme leaves, and lavender flowers into the teapot.
3. Once the water has reached a boil, pour it over the herbs in the teapot, covering them completely. Place the lid on the teapot to contain the heat and steam.
4. Allow the tea to steep for 5 minutes. This will ensure the flavors are well-infused into the water, creating a full-bodied taste. Adjust the steeping time to your preference for a stronger or more delicate flavor.
5. After steeping, place the strainer over your tea cup and pour the tea through it, capturing the leaves and flowers. This will give you a clear tea with no herbal residue.
6. If you desire a touch of sweetness, stir in a teaspoon of honey until it dissolves fully into the tea.
7. Garnish each cup with a fresh mint leaf to add a refreshing touch to your Sleepy Thyme Embrace.

DREAM WEAVER'S WILD BERRY BREW

Sip Slowly

Nestled under a canopy of stars, this Dream Weaver's Wild Berry Brew is the perfect potion to lull you into a serene slumber. Infused with a harmonious blend of wild berries and calming herbs, this tea is a gentle embrace for the soul, inviting you to unwind and drift away into a peaceful evening reverie.

2 servings   10 minutes   5 minutes

Equipment: Teapot, Measuring spoons, Strainer

Ingredients:
- 2 cups filtered water
- 2 teaspoons dried wild berries (blueberries, strawberries, raspberries)
- 1 teaspoon chamomile flowers
- 1 teaspoon lavender buds
- 1 teaspoon rose hips
- 1 teaspoon honey or maple syrup (optional for sweetness)
- lemon slices (for garnish)
- fresh mint leaves (for garnish)

Directions:
1. Bring the filtered water to a near boil in the teapot.
2. Combine dried wild berries, chamomile flowers, lavender buds, and rose hips in the teapot with hot water, and allow the blend to steep for 5 minutes, covered. This will let the flavors and calming properties of the herbs fully infuse into the brew.
3. Strain the tea into cups, making sure to catch any loose herbs or berries.
4. Stir in honey or maple syrup to each cup according to taste, if a touch of sweetness is desired.
5. Garnish each cup with a slice of lemon and a sprig of fresh mint for an additional layer of fresh, soothing flavor.

A World of Tea Recipes
Dinner Teas: Pairing with Meals

RICH LAPSANG SOUCHONG SMOKY BLEND

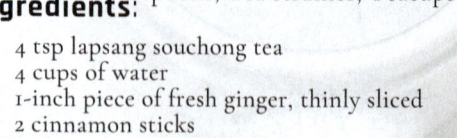

Invoke a sense of cozy campfire evenings with this boldly smoky and deeply aromatic tea. Rich Lapsang Souchong Smoky Blend melds the robust flavors of pine-smoked black tea with a hint of spice and citrus. This savory concoction is an excellent dinner companion, especially with grilled or roasted dishes, adding depth and warmth to your mealtime experience.

Equipment: Teapot or saucepan, Measuring spoons, Tea strainer, Teacups

4 servings
5 minutes
10 minutes

Ingredients:
- 4 tsp lapsang souchong tea
- 4 cups of water
- 1-inch piece of fresh ginger, thinly sliced
- 2 cinnamon sticks
- 4 cloves
- 2 star anise
- zest of 1 orange, in wide strips
- optional: honey or brown sugar to taste

Directions:
1. To begin, bring 4 cups of water to a boil in a teapot or saucepan.
2. Add the Lapsang Souchong tea leaves to the boiling water, along with the sliced ginger, cinnamon sticks, cloves, and star anise.
3. After 5–7 minutes, reduce the heat and allow the tea to simmer, facilitating the infusion of the spices' comforting, toasty flavors into the brew.
4. Meanwhile, add the orange zest strips to your tea strainer or infuser.
5. After the tea has simmered, remove it from the heat and pour it through the tea strainer or infuser into the teacups. The orange zest will add a burst of citrusy brightness as the tea passes over it.
6. If sweetness is desired, stir in honey or brown sugar according to taste.
7. Give the tea a minute or so in the teacups to marry the smoky notes with the citrus zest infusion before serving.

Enjoy yourself

BOLD MASALA CHAI FOR SPICY CUISINE

Unleash the robust flavors of Bold Masala Chai as the perfect partner to your spicy meals. This chai stands up to the heat with its own symphony of spices that will dance on your palate and complement the complexity of your spicy cuisine.

4 servings
10 minutes
20 minutes

Equipment: Medium saucepan, Fine-mesh strainer, Teapot

Ingredients:
- 4 cups water
- 2 teaspoons of loose black tea leaves or 2 black tea bags
- 1-inch piece fresh ginger, thinly sliced
- 6 green cardamom pods, lightly crushed
- 4 cloves
- 1 cinnamon stick
- 6 black peppercorns
- 2 star anise
- 1/2 teaspoon fennel seeds
- 1/4 teaspoon nutmeg, freshly grated
- 1 cup milk, whole or substitute, of your choosing
- 2-4 tablespoons sugar, honey, or sweetener of choice (adjust to taste)

Directions:
1. In a medium saucepan, bring the water to a gentle boil. Add the ginger, cardamom pods, cloves, cinnamon stick, black peppercorns, star anise, fennel seeds, and nutmeg. Simmer on low heat for 10 minutes allowing the spices to infuse their flavors into the water.
2. Black tea sachets or loose tea leaves should be added to the spiced water. Five minutes of steeping will produce a robust flavor that can withstand piquant dishes.
3. Stir the milk in a separate saucepan or microwave until it reaches a temperature of heated but not boiling, while the tea steeps.
4. After steeping the tea, remove it from heat. If using tea bags, squeeze and remove them. When using loose tea leaves, remove the seasonings and tea leaves from the tea by transferring the liquid through a fine-mesh strainer into a teapot or pitcher.
5. After combining the strained tea and heated milk, incorporate the sweetener while making any necessary adjustments to taste.
6. Serve the masala chai in individual cups immediately, ensuring each cup gets a harmonious blend of tea and spices.

DELICATE WHITE PEONY FOR LIGHT DISHES

Embrace the subtle elegance of this Delicate White Peony tea, a perfect accompaniment to your light dinner fare. With its gentle floral notes and a hint of sweetness, this tea complements dishes without overpowering them, making it an ideal beverage to serve with salads, white fish, or chicken.

Equipment: Teapot or kettle, Tea infuser or strainer, Teacups

Ingredients:

- 4 cups filtered water
- 4 tsp white peony (bai mudan) tea leaves
- optional: honey or sweetener of your choice
- optional: lemon wedges or fresh mint for garnish

4 servings
5 minutes
10 minutes

Directions:

1. Begin by bringing the filtered water to just short of a boil, around 180°F to 185°F. Overheating the water can lead to bitterness in the delicate white tea, so use a thermometer if possible.
2. Place the White Peony tea leaves into the tea infuser or strainer.
3. Before placing the tea leaves in the water, ensure that they are completely submerged.
4. Delay brewing the tea for five to seven minutes. In contrast to black tea, white tea ought to be steeped for a shorter duration than green tea in order to fully extract its flavor characteristic.
5. After steeping, remove the tea leaves by lifting out the infuser or straining the tea into each cup.
6. Alternately, a minor quantity of honey or an alternative sweetening agent may be utilized to augment the tea's inherent sweetness.
7. Serve immediately, garnishing with a lemon wedge or a sprig of fresh mint if desired.

SAVORY SAGE GREEN TEA

Tea Time

Take your dinner experience to a new level with Savory Sage Green Tea—a warm, earthy fusion that complements a variety of savory dishes. This flavorful beverage is perfect for sipping alongside your meal, enhancing and balancing the complex flavors of your dinner.

4 servings   10 minutes   5 minutes

Equipment: Teapot or saucepan, Fine-mesh strainer, Tea cups

Ingredients:

- 4 cups water
- 4 tsp green tea leaves
- 8 fresh sage leaves
- 2 tbsp honey (or to taste)
- 4 lemon wedges (for garnish)
- optional: a pinch of black pepper

Directions:

1. Heat water in a teapot or saucepan to just short of boiling (about 80°C or 175°F) to ensure the green tea leaves do not burn, which can make the tea taste bitter.
2. Stew the green tea leaves in the heated water for a duration of two minutes.
3. Transfer the sage leaves to the teapot containing the steeping green tea after delicately crushing them with your fingers to extract their essential oils.
4. Allow the sage leaves to infuse with the green tea for an additional 3 minutes.
5. Strain the tea mixture through a fine-mesh strainer into tea cups to remove the leaves.
6. To each cup, add honey to taste to temper the savory sage flavor.
7. If you like a little more complexity, add a small pinch of black pepper to each cup and stir well.
8. Garnish each tea cup with a lemon wedge, which can be squeezed into the tea to add a fresh, zesty note.

HEARTY ROASTED OOLONG FOR GRILLED FOODS

A robust roasted Oolong tea that pairs well with the smokey tastes of grilled meats and vegetables. Its robust character and woody notes bring out the best in hearty meals without overpowering the palette.

Equipment: Tea kettle, Teapot, Measuring spoons, Strainer

Ingredients:

- 4 teaspoons high-quality roasted oolong tea leaves (or 4 tea bags)
- 1 liter fresh, filtered water
- optional: lemon slices, for garnish
- optional for a sweet touch: honey or brown sugar to taste

4 servings

10 minutes

5 minutes

Directions:

1. Begin by heating the fresh, filtered water in your tea kettle or saucepan until it is just below boiling, around 195°F (90°C). Oolong tea should not be made with boiling water as it can burn the leaves and spoil the flavor.
2. Place the roasted Oolong tea leaves into the teapot. If using tea bags, place one bag for each serving into the teapot.
3. Once the water has reached the necessary temperature, pour it over the tea leaves or bags into the teapot.
4. Allow 4-5 minutes for the tea to steep, depending on how strong you like your brew. Over-steeping might result in bitterness.
5. If you used loose leaf tea, strain the leaves from the infusion into a heat-resistant pitcher or directly into teacups. If you've used bags, simply remove them from the teapot.
6. Taste the tea and add honey or brown sugar if a sweeter flavor is desired.

Zen Sip

ELEGANT JASMINE HARMONY FOR ASIAN FARE

Elegant Jasmine Harmony for Asian Fare is a delicate tea blend perfect for complementing the intricate flavors of Asian cuisine. Its floral notes and subtle sweetness create a soothing backdrop for a diverse range of dishes, from spicy stir-fries to umami-rich sushi.

4 servings   10 minutes   5 minutes

Equipment: Teapot, Fine Mesh Strainer, Kettle

Ingredients:

- 4 cups filtered water
- 2 tablespoons quality jasmine green tea leaves
- 2 teaspoons dried chrysanthemum flowers (optional for added floral notes)
- 1 tablespoon honey (or to taste, optional for sweetness)
- fresh jasmine blossoms for garnish (ensure they are pesticide-free and suitable for consumption)

Directions:

1. To avoid bitterness, bring the filtered water to a slow simmer in the kettle, without surpassing 180°F (82°C).
2. Add the jasmine green tea leaves and dried chrysanthemum flowers (if using) to the teapot.
3. Pour the heated water into the teapot and steep the tea for 3 to 4 minutes. Avoid steeping the tea for too long as this can turn it bitter.
4. Pour the tea into cups using the fine mesh strainer, making sure to catch any loose leaves or blossoms.
5. If desired, stir in a teaspoon of honey into each cup for a touch of sweetness that complements the floral undertones.
6. Garnish each cup with a fresh jasmine blossom on the rim or floating in the tea.

ZESTY LEMON-GINGER DETOX FOR CLEANSING

Embark on a rejuvenating journey with the Zesty Lemon-Ginger Detox for Cleansing. This invigorating blend combines the tangy freshness of lemon with the warm, spicy undertones of ginger, creating a revitalizing infusion perfect for complementing a balanced meal or enjoying as a purifying post-dinner ritual.

Equipment: Teapot, Strainer, Measuring spoons, Knife, Cutting board

Ingredients:
- 4 cups water
- 2 inches fresh ginger root, thinly sliced
- 2 organic lemons (1 juiced and 1 thinly sliced)
- 1 tbsp honey, or to taste
- a pinch of cayenne pepper (optional)
- fresh mint leaves for garnish (optional)

4 servings
5 minutes
15 minutes

Directions:
1. Place the four cups of water in a teapot or saucepan and bring to a rolling simmer.
2. Allow the thinly sliced ginger to simmer in the boiling water for 10 minutes to absorb all of its fiery qualities.
3. After simmering, remove from heat and add the juice of one lemon to the infusion, stirring well to combine.
4. Permit the mixture to percolate for an additional five minutes, facilitating the fusion of flavors and establishing a cohesive blend.
5. Add a sprinkle of cayenne pepper to the tea, if desired, to increase its warming and detoxifying properties.
6. Use a strainer to pour the tea into individual cups, avoiding ginger slices and any lemon seeds.
7. Sweeten each cup with a teaspoon of honey, or adjust according to your taste.
8. Garnish with a slice of lemon and a few fresh mint leaves to enhance the tea's aroma and visual appeal.

Tea Delight

SOPHISTICATED EARL GREY FOR EUROPEAN CUISINE

Immerse yourself in the refined flavors of a Sophisticated Earl Grey, crafted to complement and enhance the rich tapestry of European cuisine. This elegant tea blend offers a harmonious balance of citrus notes from bergamot, the spicy warmth of vanilla, and the depth of lavender to elegantly round out an upscale dinner experience.

4 servings   5 minutes   5 minutes

Equipment: Teapot, Kettle, Measuring spoons, Tea strainer

Ingredients:
- 4 teaspoons loose leaf earl grey tea
- 4 cups boiling water
- 2 teaspoons dried lavender flowers
- 1 vanilla pod, split and seeds scraped
- 1 tablespoon honey (optional)
- 4 slices of lemon (for garnish)
- sprig of fresh lavender (for garnish)

Directions:
1. Preheat your teapot by swirling a bit of boiling water in it and then discard the water. This will help to maintain the temperature while the tea steeps.
2. Place the loose leaf Earl Grey tea, dried lavender flowers, and split and scraped seeds of the vanilla pod into the teapot.
3. Depending on the desired strength, pour 4 glasses of boiling water over the tea blend and allow it to steep for 3 to 5 minutes.
4. While your tea is steeping, warm the cups by rinsing them with hot water.
5. After steeping, strain the tea into the warmed cups, ensuring none of the leaves or flowers make it into the poured tea.
6. If desired, sweeten each cup with a teaspoon of honey to bring out the complex flavors of the bergamot and vanilla.
7. For an exquisite finishing touch, garnish each cup with a lemon slice and a sprig of fresh lavender.

WARMING CINNAMON PU-ERH

Warming Cinnamon Pu-erh is an earthy and spiced tea that complements robust dinner flavors, especially grilled meats or hearty stews. The deep, fermented character of Pu-erh tea is beautifully accentuated with the spicy warmth of cinnamon, creating a beverage that is both soothing and invigorating.

Equipment: Teapot, Tea strainer or infuser, Kettle, Measuring spoons

Ingredients:
- 1 tablespoon pu-erh tea leaves
- 4 cups water
- 2 cinnamon sticks
- optional: 1 tablespoon honey or to taste

4 servings
5 minutes
10 minutes

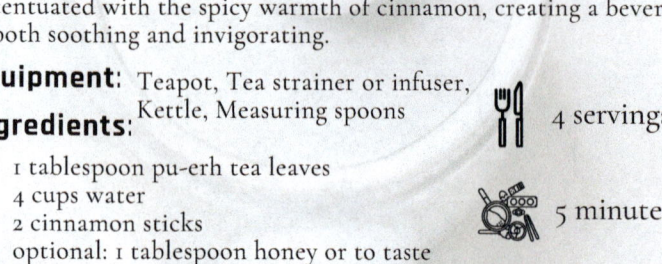

Directions:
1. Bring water to a boil in the kettle. While waiting for the water to heat, place the Pu-erh tea leaves and cinnamon sticks into the teapot.
2. Once the water reaches boiling, pour it over the tea leaves and cinnamon sticks in the teapot.
3. Cover the teapot and let the tea steep for 5-7 minutes, depending on how strong you prefer your tea.
4. Remove the cinnamon sticks and tea leaves using a strainer or infuser.
5. If desired, sweeten the tea with honey to your preferred taste.
6. Pour the tea into individual cups, making sure to leave room for any additions or to savor the tea as it is.

Sip Slowly

REFRESHING MINT AND CUCUMBER GREEN TEA

Indulge in the soothing calm of this Refreshing Mint and Cucumber Green Tea, a perfect accompanist to your dinner. This blend harmonizes the warmth of green tea with the coolness of fresh cucumber and mint, creating a beverage that both relaxes and revitalizes. The subtle taste profile makes it an ideal companion for light salads, seafood, or a simple pastel dish.

4 servings   10 minutes   5 minutes

Equipment: Teapot, Fine mesh strainer, Pitcher, Spoon, Knife, Cutting board

Ingredients:
- 4 cups water
- 2-3 green tea bags or 2-3 teaspoons of loose-leaf green tea
- 1/2 cucumber, thinly sliced
- 1/4 cup fresh mint leaves, roughly torn or chopped
- 2 tbsp honey or to taste (optional)
- ice cubes (for serving)
- additional cucumber slices and mint leaves for garnish (optional)

Directions:
1. Begin by boiling the water in your teapot or saucepan. Once it reaches a near boil, remove it from the heat to prevent the green tea from becoming bitter.
2. Steep the green tea bags or loose-leaf tea in the hot water for 3 minutes. If you're using a teapot with an infuser, place the tea directly into it. If using a saucepan, you can later strain the leaves out.
3. Add the cucumber slices that have been thinly sliced and the fresh mint leaves to the pitcher or serving container while the tea steeps.
4. Remove the tea bags or filter the loose leaves once the tea has steeped, and pour the hot tea over the cucumber and mint.. Let the fusion of flavors take place as the mixture cools down for about 2-3 minutes.
5. If you prefer a sweeter tea, now is the time to stir in the honey until well dissolved.
6. Place the pitcher in the refrigerator to chill, or if serving immediately, add plenty of ice cubes to cool the tea quickly.
7. Once the tea is well chilled, give it a gentle stir and pour into glasses over additional ice cubes, if desired.
8. Just prior to serving, adorn each glass with an additional cucumber slice and a sprig of mint to augment the aesthetic appeal and introduce a revitalizing fragrance.

FLORAL HIBISCUS BLISS FOR TROPICAL MEALS

A vibrant and tangy concoction, the Floral Hibiscus Bliss is the perfect pairing for your sumptuous tropical dinners. Infused with the exotic notes of hibiscus, a hint of sweet citrus, and an aromatic whiff of fresh mint, this tea is a delightful symphony of flavors that can complement the bold and spicy elements of tropical cuisine.

Equipment: Teapot or saucepan, Fine mesh strainer

Ingredients:

- 4 cups water
- 1/4 cup dried hibiscus flowers
- 3 tbsp honey (or to taste)
- 1 medium orange (juice and zest)
- 1 tsp fresh ginger, finely grated
- fresh mint leaves (for garnish)
- optional: cinnamon stick for an extra layer of warmth

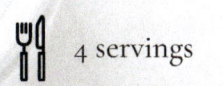

4 servings
10 minutes
15 minutes

Directions:

1. Bring water to a rolling boil in your teapot or saucepan.
2. Once the water has come to a boil, reduce the heat and add the dried hibiscus flowers and the optional cinnamon stick if desired. Allow the mixture to simmer for 10 minutes.
3. Meanwhile, zest the orange and then squeeze to get the fresh juice.
4. After the hibiscus has steeped for 10 minutes, remove from the heat and strain the tea to eliminate the hibiscus flowers and any other solids.
5. Stir in the honey while the tea is still warm so that it dissolves easily.
6. Add in the freshly grated ginger and stir in the orange juice and zest for a citrusy punch.
7. Let the tea cool for a few minutes if you prefer to serve it warm, or chill in the refrigerator if desired as a refreshing cold beverage.
8. Serve the Floral Hibiscus Bliss in individual cups or glasses, garnished with fresh mint leaves.

Enjoy yourself

ROBUST YUNNAN BLACK TEA FOR RICH FOODS

Enjoy the luxury of a full-bodied Yunnan black tea, with its malty flavors and hints of chocolate, perfectly tailored to complement rich, hearty meals. This bold brew stands up to the complexity of intense dishes, balancing and enhancing your dining experience.

4 servings   5 minutes   5 minutes

Equipment: Teapot, Tea strainer or infuser, Kettle

Ingredients:

- 4 cups water
- 2-3 green tea bags or 2-3 teaspoons of loose-leaf green tea
- 1/2 cucumber, thinly sliced
- 1/4 cup fresh mint leaves, roughly torn or chopped
- 2 tbsp honey or to taste (optional)
- ice cubes (for serving)
- additional cucumber slices and mint leaves for garnish (optional)

Directions:

1. Begin by bringing the 4 cups of water to a boil in your kettle. Yunnan black tea is best brewed with water temperature just off the boil, around 200°F to 212°F.
2. Warm the teapot by rinsing it with hot water to ensure your tea stays warm during the steeping process.
3. Add the Yunnan black tea leaves to the teapot or place them into your tea strainer or infuser.
4. Once the water has reached the correct temperature, pour it over the tea leaves in the teapot and place the lid on.
5. Steep the tea for 3-5 minutes. The longer you steep, the stronger and more robust the flavor will become.
6. If using a tea strainer or infuser, remove it from the pot after the desired steeping time.
7. Serve the hot brewed tea into individual cups. If you prefer, you can offer lemon wedges or milk for guests to add to their tea, along with a sweetener if desired.

SOOTHING LAVENDER GREY FOR AFTER-DINNER RELAXATION

Unwind after a fulfilling dinner with the calming fragrance of lavender blended seamlessly with the citrusy spark of Earl Grey. Our Soothing Lavender Grey is a symphony of aromatic bliss that promises to relax your senses and digestifs alike. It's the perfect closing number to your meal's gastronomic concert, gently easing you into an evening of peaceful respite or engaging conversation.

Equipment: Teapot, Measuring spoons, Kettle, Tea cups

Ingredients:
- 4 teaspoons earl grey tea leaves
- 1 tablespoon dried lavender flowers
- 4 cups filtered water
- 1 teaspoon honey, or to taste (optional)
- lemon slices or zest for garnish (optional)

4 servings
5 minutes
10 minutes

Directions:
1. Heat the filtered water in your kettle until it is just about to boil.
2. While the water is heating, add the Earl Grey tea leaves and dried lavender flowers to the teapot.
3. Once the water has reached the right temperature, pour it over the tea leaves and lavender in the teapot.
4. Steep for approximately 3-4 minutes, depending on your taste preference for strength.
5. Strain the tea into each tea cup, ensuring the lavender and tea leaves remain in the teapot.
6. If desired, sweeten each serving with a teaspoon of honey to draw out the complex floral and citrus notes.
7. Garnish with a thin slice of lemon or a sprinkle of lemon zest to add a bright, refreshing layer to the palette.

Tea Time

CITRUS BURST DARJEELING FOR SEAFOOD

This fresh and aromatic tea blend combines the uplifting notes of citrus with the delicate, musky flavor of Darjeeling, creating a perfect accompaniment to a variety of seafood dishes. The subtle astringency cuts through the richness of seafood, while the zesty infusion enhances its natural flavors.

4 servings   10 minutes   7 minutes

Equipment: Teapot, Kettle, Tea infuser or strainer, Measuring spoon

Ingredients:
- 4 teaspoons darjeeling tea leaves
- 1 tablespoon fresh orange zest
- 1 tablespoon fresh lemon zest
- 4 cups filtered water
- optional: honey or sugar to taste
- optional: fresh mint leaves for garnish

Directions:
1. Heat water in a kettle until it reaches just below the boiling point, around 200°F (93°C). This temperature will extract the flavors without scorching the delicate tea leaves.
2. In the meantime, mix the fresh orange and lemon zest with the Darjeeling tea leaves, allowing the citrus oils to lightly coat the tea.
3. Place the tea and zest mixture into your tea infuser or directly into the teapot if you plan to strain it later.
4. Pour the heated water over the Darjeeling and citrus mixture and steep for 3 to 4 minutes. Be careful not to over-steep, as this may result in a bitter taste, masking the delicate notes of the tea and citrus.
5. After steeping, remove the tea infuser or strain the tea to remove the leaves and zest.
6. Sweeten with honey or sugar if desired, stirring gently to combine.
7. Serve the tea hot, in pre-warmed cups.
8. If you prefer, garnish with a sprig of fresh mint for an additional pop of color and a refreshing twist.

SPICE MARKET HERBAL INFUSION

Embark on an exotic journey with every sip of Spice Market Herbal Infusion, a caffeine-free blend that captures the vibrant essence of a bustling spice market. This bold, aromatic tea harmonizes savory and sweet spices, perfect for complementing a wide array of dinner courses, from Middle Eastern cuisines to hearty stews.

Equipment: Teapot with infuser, Kettle, Measuring spoons

Ingredients:

- 1/4 cup dried chamomile flowers
- 2 tbsp dried mint leaves
- 1 tbsp fennel seeds
- 1 tbsp cardamom pods, crushed
- 1 tsp cinnamon chips
- 1/2 tsp black peppercorns, lightly crushed
- 1/4 tsp clove buds
- 1/2-inch piece fresh ginger, thinly sliced
- 4 cups boiling water
- optional: honey or your choice of sweetener, to taste

4 servings

5 minutes

10 minutes

Directions:

1. Bring water to a rolling boil in the kettle.
2. Combine the dried chamomile, mint leaves, fennel seeds, crushed cardamom pods, cinnamon chips, crushed peppercorns, clove buds, and sliced ginger in the infuser of your teapot.
3. Once the water has reached the boiling point, slowly pour it over the herbs and spices in the infuser, ensuring all elements are fully submerged.
4. Allow the infusion to steep for 10 minutes, covered. The longer it steeps, the more apparent the flavors become, so alter the steeping time according to whether you prefer a stronger or softer infusion.
5. Carefully remove the infuser or strain the tea after steeping to separate the liquid from the spices and herbs.
6. Taste and add honey or your preferred sweetener if desired. Stir until well combined.

SMOKED CHERRY WOOD BLACK TEA

Zen Sip

Savor the rich, aromatic flavors of a Smoked Cherry Wood Black Tea, designed to complement robust dinner courses. This luxurious brew combines the depth of black tea with the fine smokiness imparted from real cherry wood. Perfect for elevating any meal, it's a tea that stands up to hearty dishes and engages the senses with its complex profile.

4 servings   15 minutes   10 minutes

Equipment: Teapot, Tea kettle, Heat-resistant pitcher, Fine mesh strainer

Ingredients:

- 4 cups filtered water
- 4 tbsp loose leaf black tea, of a high-quality, strong variety
- 1 cherry wood plank, small enough to fit within the heat-resistant pitcher
- honey or sweetener of choice is optional.

Directions:

1. Begin by heating the filtered water in the tea kettle until it reaches a rolling boil.
2. While the water is heating, place the cherry wood plank at the bottom of the heat-resistant pitcher.
3. Once the water has boiled, gently pour it over the cherry wood plank, allowing it to steep and infuse the water with smoky notes for about 5 minutes.
4. Place the loose leaf black tea in the teapot.
5. Remove the cherry wood plank with tongs and discard. Pour the smoked water into the teapot over the black tea leaves.
6. Allow 3-5 minutes for the tea to steep, depending on how strong you want your tea.
7. Strain the tea into cups, leaving the tea leaves behind.
8. If desired, sweeten each serving to taste with honey or your preferred sweetener.

ARTISANAL BERGAMOT AND ROSE HIP BLEND

Unlock a world of aromatic flourish with this bespoke blend of citrusy bergamot and tart rose hips, perfect for enriching your dinner experience. The Artisanal Bergamot and Rose Hip Blend is a delicate dance of flavors designed to complement the savory notes of your evening meal, bringing a soothing balance to your palate.

Equipment: Teapot or infuser, Kettle, Measuring spoons

Ingredients:

- 4 cups filtered water
- 2 tbsp dried rose hips
- 1 tbsp black tea leaves, high-quality, preferably loose
- 1 tsp dried bergamot orange peel (or the zest of 1 fresh bergamot, if available)
- honey or sweetener of choice, to taste

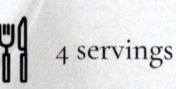

4 servings
5 minutes
10 minutes

Directions:

1. Begin by bringing the filtered water to a near boiling point using your kettle.
2. In the teapot or infuser, combine the dried rose hips, black tea leaves, and dried bergamot orange peel. If using a zester, zest the bergamot directly into the teapot or infuser for the freshest flavor.
3. Once the water has reached the right temperature, pour it over the mixed ingredients, making sure they are fully submerged and can infuse evenly.
4. Allow the blend to steep for approximately 5-7 minutes. This will vary depending on how strong you prefer your tea. For a milder brew, limit the steeping time.
5. Strain the tea into cups, ensuring that the rose hips and tea leaves remain in the teapot/in the infuser.
6. If you prefer a touch of sweetness to your tea, add honey or your chosen sweetener to taste, stirring gently until dissolved.

Tea Delight

FRAGRANT LEMONGRASS AND BASIL TISANE

Experience a symphony of flavors with this Fragrant Lemongrass and Basil Tisane, perfect for a tranquil dinner setting. Its aromatic properties will enhance your meal with a refreshing yet soothing touch, complementing zesty or lightly spiced dishes beautifully.

4 servings   10 minutes   15 minutes

Equipment: Teapot or Large Pitcher, Kettle, Fine Mesh Strainer

Ingredients:

- 1 stalk fresh lemongrass, smashed and cut into 2-inch pieces
- 1/4 cup fresh basil leaves, tightly packed
- 4 cups filtered water
- 2 tbsp honey, or to taste (optional)
- 4 slices lemon (optional for garnish)
- fresh basil sprigs (optional for garnish)

Directions:

1. Begin by boiling the filtered water in your kettle.
2. Meanwhile, prepare your lemongrass by removing the outer layer and smashing the stalk with the back of a knife to release its fragrant oils. Then, cut it into 2-inch pieces.
3. Place the lemongrass pieces and fresh basil leaves in the teapot or pitcher.
4. Once the water reaches a rolling boil, pour it over the lemongrass and basil leaves in the pot or pitcher.
5. Allow the mixture to steep for about 10 to 15 minutes, depending on how strong a flavor you prefer.
6. After the steeping process, pour the infusion through a fine mesh strainer into cups or mugs to remove the leaves and lemongrass pieces.
7. If desired, sweeten your Lemongrass and Basil Tisane with honey, stirring until it's well dissolved.
8. Garnish each cup with a slice of lemon and a sprig of fresh basil for an extra touch of elegance and flavor.

SWEET LYCHEE BLACK TEA FOR DESSERT PAIRING

This Sweet Lychee Black Tea is the perfect accompaniment to end a luxurious meal, balancing rich and decadent desserts with its fragrant and slightly floral sweetness. The luscious taste of ripe lychee infuses beautifully with the boldness of black tea, creating a delightful sensory experience unlike any other.

Equipment: Teapot, Small saucepan, Fine-mesh strainer

Ingredients:

- 4 cups Water
- 4 Black tea bags or 4 teaspoons loose-leaf black tea
- 1/2 cup Canned lychees in syrup
- Fresh lychees for garnish (optional)
- 2 tablespoons Honey (or to taste)
- Edible rose petals for garnish (optional)

4 servings
10 minutes
5 minutes

Directions:

1. Begin by bringing the water to a boil in a small saucepan.
2. Once boiling, remove from heat and add the black tea bags or loose-leaf black tea. Steep the tea for 3-5 minutes, depending on how strong you like your tea. Remove the tea bags or strain the loose leaves after steeping.
3. While the tea is still hot, add the canned lychees along with 2 tablespoons of lychee syrup from the can. Allow the lychees to infuse the tea for an additional 2 minutes.
4. Stir in honey to sweeten the tea. Adjust according to your preference for sweetness.
5. Using a fine-mesh strainer, pour the tea into individual serving cups, ensuring that any tea leaves or lychee pieces are caught in the strainer.
6. If desired, garnish each cup with a fresh lychee and a sprinkle of edible rose petals for an added touch of elegance.

Sip Slowly

FENNEL AND ANISE DIGESTIF HERBAL TEA

This soothing Fennel and Anise Digestif Herbal Tea is a perfect after-dinner beverage. With notes of sweet anise and a gentle hint of earthy fennel, this tea aids digestion and offers a moment of calm relaxation. Its aromatic qualities make it an enchanting way to end any culinary experience.

4 servings   5 minutes   10 minutes

Equipment: Teapot, Tea strainer, Kettle

Ingredients:

- 1 tablespoon Dried fennel seeds
- 1 tablespoon Dried anise seeds
- 4 cups Boiling water
- 1 teaspoon Honey, or to taste (optional)
- 1 Fresh mint leaf (for garnish)

Directions:

1. Place the fennel and anise seeds into the teapot.
2. Boil the 4 cups of water using your kettle.
3. Once the water reaches a rolling boil, carefully pour it over the seeds in the teapot.
4. Cover the teapot and let the mix steep for about 8-10 minutes, depending on how strong you prefer the flavors.
5. While waiting, if desired, you can rinse teacups with hot water to warm them. This helps in keeping the tea hot while serving.
6. After steeping, strain the tea through a tea strainer into each cup to remove the seeds.
7. If sweetening is preferred, add a teaspoon of honey to each cup and stir gently to incorporate.
8. Garnish each cup with a mint leaf, adding a refreshing touch to the warm drink.

CARAMELIZED HONEY ROOIBOS FOR COMFORTING EVENINGS

Escape into a soothing evening with Caramelized Honey Rooibos, a warm, sweet, and earthy elixir that pairs magnificently with hearty meals. It promotes relaxation while its gentle, aromatic sweetness offers a complement to savory dishes, making it an ideal end to your day.

Equipment: Saucepan, Whisk, Measuring Cups and Spoons, Tea Strainer or Infuser

Ingredients:
- 4 cups water
- 4 tbsp loose leaf rooibos tea or 4 rooibos tea bags
- 1/4 cup honey
- 2 tbsp brown sugar
- 1 cinnamon stick
- 1 teaspoon vanilla extract or 1/2 vanilla bean, split and scraped
- whipped cream (optional for garnish)
- cinnamon powder (optional for garnish)

4 servings
10 minutes
15 minutes

Enjoy yourself

Directions:
1. In a saucepan, bring the water to a boil. When the water is boiling, add the Rooibos tea leaves, either directly or through an infuser. Reduce the heat to low, cover, and leave to simmer for 5 minutes.
2. Consolidate the honey and brown sugar in an individual small saucepan over medium heat, while the tea steeps. Three to four minutes, while whisking continuously, bring the mixture to a full boil and transform it into something that resembles caramelized sugar.
3. Carefully pour the caramelized honey mixture into the steeping tea (remove tea leaves or bags first if necessary) and add the cinnamon stick and vanilla bean scrapings or vanilla extract. Allow it to simmer for another 5 minutes for the flavors to infuse.
4. Strain the tea into cups or a teapot to eliminate any solids, including the vanilla bean pod and cinnamon stick, after removing from heat.
5. For added comfort, one may garnish the tea with a dollop of whipped cream and a dusting of cinnamon powder, if desired.

VANILLA ORCHID BLACK TEA FOR SOPHISTICATED PALATES

A refined and fragrant tea blend with the powerful flavors of black tea, the sweet, creamy essence of vanilla, and the gentle floral notes of orchid. The perfect accompaniment to an elegant dinner, this tea delights the senses and complements a wide range of savory dishes.

4 servings   5 minutes   5 minutes

Equipment: Teapot, Measuring spoons, Strainer (if using loose tea), Teacups

Ingredients:
- 4 cups filtered water
- fourth teaspoon of black tea leaves (or four teabags of premium black tea)
- 1 vanilla pod, split lengthwise (or 1 tsp of pure vanilla extract)
- 1 tsp dried orchid petals (optional, for a more floral note)
- 1 tbsp honey or to taste (optional, for sweetness)
- 4-6 fresh mint leaves (for garnish, optional)

Directions:
1. In a kettle, bring the filtered water to a rolling simmer.
2. Place the black tea leaves, split vanilla pod, and dried orchid petals in the teapot.
3. Once the water reaches a boil, pour it over the tea blend in the teapot.
4. Cover and steep for about 4 minutes. This allows the tea to fully infuse with the flavors of vanilla and orchid. In lieu of utilizing a capsule, it is advisable to add vanilla extract to the tea after it has steeped, so as to safeguard its delicate flavor.
5. While the tea steeps, place a strainer over each teacup to catch the tea leaves and petals.
6. After steeping, pour the tea through the strainer into each teacup.
7. If desired, sweeten each cup with a teaspoon of honey, or to taste.
8. Garnish each cup with a mint leaf or two for a fresh touch.

A World of Tea Recipes

Special Occasions: Celebratory and Seasonal Teas

FESTIVE WINTER SPICE TEA

As snow blankets the ground and a chill hangs in the air, wrap your hands around a steaming mug of Festive Winter Spice Tea. This heartwarming brew intertwines the classic flavors of the season with a welcoming, spiced aroma, making it the perfect accompaniment to your winter festivities. Citrusy notes dance with a symphony of spices, bringing warmth and cheer to any holiday gathering or cozy night in.

Equipment: Medium Saucepan, Fine Mesh Strainer, Teapot or Serving Jug

4 servings
10 minutes
20 minutes

Ingredients:
- 4 cups water
- 4 bags black tea (or 4 teaspoons of loose-leaf black tea)
- 1 orange, zested and juiced
- 2 cinnamon sticks
- 8 whole cloves
- 4 star anise
- 1-inch piece fresh ginger, thinly sliced
- prefer a desired level of sweetness; 1/4 cup honey or maple syrup may be substituted.
- fresh orange slices, for garnish
- cinnamon sticks, for garnish

Enjoy yourself

Directions:
1. Bring the 4 cups of water to a gentle boil in a medium saucepan.
2. Reduce the heat to low and add the black tea, orange zest, orange juice, cinnamon sticks, whole cloves, star anise, and sliced ginger to the water.
3. Simmer the mixture for 15 minutes, making sure it stays below a rolling boil to avoid over-extracting the tea and making it bitter.
4. Once the liquid has reached a simmer, remove the saucepan from the heat and let it infuse for an additional five minutes.
5. Pour the tea into a preheated teapot or serving container via a fine mesh strainer, ensuring to remove any solid particles.
6. If desirable, incorporate honey or maple syrup while adjusting the sweetness to personal taste.
7. Pour the tea into individual cups or mugs, and garnish each with a fresh orange slice and a cinnamon stick.

SPRING CHERRY BLOSSOM CELEBRATION

Embrace the essence of spring with a delicate tea named "Spring Cherry Blossom Celebration" – a blend that captures the ephemeral beauty of cherry blossoms in a cup. This tea combines the floral grace of cherry blossoms with the refreshing zest of green tea, creating a medley that is perfect for welcoming the new season or celebrating moments of renewal and joy.

Equipment: Teapot, Tea infuser or strainer, Kettle, Measuring spoons

Ingredients:
- 4 tsp. sencha or any mild green tea
- 2 cups hot water (not boiling, approx. 175°f/80°c)
- 1 tbsp. dried cherry blossoms (salt-pickled, with the salt washed off)
- 2 tbsp. cherry syrup
- fresh cherry blossoms for garnish (optional, ensure they are pesticide-free)
- ice cubes (if serving cold)

4 servings   15 minutes   5 minutes

Directions:
1. Pre-rinse the dried cherry blossoms to remove the salt and place them into the teapot.
2. Heat the water to the recommended temperature and pour over the cherry blossoms in the teapot.
3. Add the green tea to the teapot, either directly or using an infuser, and allow the mixture to steep for about 3 minutes.
4. Prepare the serving glasses or cups by adding 1/2 tablespoon of cherry syrup to each while the tea steeps.
5. Strain the tea mixture, pouring it equally into the prepared glasses or cups, letting the syrup mix with the tea. For an iced version, fill the glasses with ice before pouring the tea.
6. If using, delicately garnish each serving with a fresh cherry blossom on top.

SUMMER SOLSTICE ICED BERRY BLEND

Celebrate the peak of summer with this refreshing and vibrant Summer Solstice Iced Berry Blend. On the longest day of the year, this delectable concoction combines the natural sweetness of summer berries with the understated sophistication of white tea to produce the ideal beverage. Its ruby-red hue and fruity aroma make for a festive and hydrating beverage that embodies the essence of summer.

Equipment: Large Pitcher, Spoon, Fine Mesh Strainer, Knife, Cutting Board

6 servings
15 minutes
0 minutes

Ingredients:
- 4 teaspoons white tea leaves
- 4 cups boiling water (approximately 80°c or 175°f to avoid scorching the tea)
- hulled and divided fresh strawberries, each 1/2 cup
- 1/2 cup fresh raspberries
- 1/2 cup fresh blueberries
- honey or agave syrup to taste (optional)
- fresh mint leaves for garnish
- ice cubes

Tea Time

Directions:
1. Place white tea leaves in the large pitcher and pour in the boiling water. Steep the tea leaves for 4 to 5 minutes. Be careful not to oversteep, as this can make the tea bitter.
2. While the tea is steeping, gently wash the berries and prepare them by cutting strawberries into halves.
3. After preparing the desired steeped tea, remove the tea leaves using a strainer, reserving any remaining infused tea in the pitcher (although some individuals may prefer to percolate the tea directly into the pitcher).
4. After bringing the tea to room temperature, chill it in the refrigerator for one to two hours, or until completely cooled.
5. When the tea is chilled, add the berries to the pitcher, stirring gently to combine. If you prefer a subtly sweeter drink, stir in the desired amount of honey or agave syrup until well dissolved.
6. After placing ice crystals in each glass, drizzle the berry blend over them.
7. Elevate the ambiance and sophistication of each glass by garnishing them with fresh mint leaves.
8. Serve the Summer Solstice Iced Berry Blend immediately to bask in the full flavor of the seasonal berries and fragrant white tea.

AUTUMN HARVEST PUMPKIN CHAI

Embrace the essence of spring with a delicate tea named "Spring Cherry Blossom Celebration" – a blend that captures the ephemeral beauty of cherry blossoms in a cup. This tea combines the floral grace of cherry blossoms with the refreshing zest of green tea, creating a medley that is perfect for welcoming the new season or celebrating moments of renewal and joy.

4 servings   15 minutes   10 minutes

Equipment: Medium-sized saucepan, Whisk, Mesh strainer, Mugs

Ingredients:
- 2 cups water
- two black tea packages or two teaspoons black tea with loose leaves
- 1 cup milk (dairy or plant-based)
- pumpkin purée, 1/2 cup (excluding pie filling)
- 2 tablespoons brown sugar (or to taste)
- 1 teaspoon vanilla extract
- 1/4 teaspoon ground cinnamon
- 1/4 teaspoon ground ginger
- 1/8 teaspoon ground cloves
- 1/8 teaspoon ground nutmeg
- pinch of salt
- whipped cream (optional, for garnish)
- cinnamon sticks (optional, for garnish)

Directions:
1. In the saucepan, bring the water to a slight boil. Add the black tea and remove from heat. After steeping the tea for approximately five minutes, remove the tea bags or strain the tea leaves.
2. Return the saucepan to low heat and whisk in the milk, pumpkin puree, brown sugar, vanilla extract, cinnamon, ginger, cloves, nutmeg, and a pinch of salt. Keep whisking occasionally to make sure everything blends smoothly.
3. Continue to heat the mixture until it's hot, but not boiling, for about 5 minutes. Pay attention as it heats to ensure it doesn't come to a boil or burn on the bottom.
4. Once hot, use a mesh strainer to pour the chai into mugs, holding back any large particles for a smooth texture.
5. Garnish each mug with a dollop of whipped cream and a sprinkle of cinnamon, or add a cinnamon stick for a festive touch.

NEW YEAR'S SPARKLING TEA TOAST

Welcome the New Year with a clink of your glass filled with New Year's Sparkling Tea Toast. This festive beverage combines the elegance of a traditional toast with the comforting warmth of tea, touched by a bubbly twist to celebrate fresh beginnings. Delightfully effervescent, it's the perfect way to raise a toast to the promise of the year ahead.

Equipment: Saucepan, Measuring Cups, Measuring Spoons, Six Champagne Flutes

Ingredients:
- 3 cups water
- 2 black tea bags or 2 tbsp loose leaf black tea
- 1/2 cup granulated sugar
- 1 orange, zested
- 1 bottle chilled sparkling white grape juice or non-alcoholic sparkling wine
- fresh mint leaves, for garnish
- orange slices, for garnish
- edible gold glitter or gold sugar (optional), for rimming the glasses

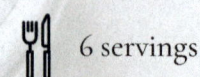

6 servings
10 minutes
5 minutes

Zen Sip

Directions:
1. Bring the water to a boil in a medium saucepan and steep the black tea for the necessary time according to the tea type, which is usually 3 to 5 minutes. Set the tea bags or loose leaves aside to cool slightly.
2. While the tea is still warm, add the granulated sugar and orange zest, stirring until the sugar is completely dissolved, creating a sweetened tea syrup.
3. Drain the syrup until it reaches ambient temperature. Refrigerate the syrup once it has cooled until it is time to serve.
4. Just before serving, prepare the glasses by moistening the rims with a little water or an orange slice and dipping them into the edible gold glitter or gold sugar, if using, to create a festive rim.
5. Distribute the chilled tea syrup evenly among the six champagne flutes.
6. Carefully fill the remainder of each glass with chilled sparkling white grape juice or non-alcoholic sparkling wine, allowing the fizz to settle and then topping up as needed. The ratio should be one part tea syrup to three parts sparkling liquid.
7. Gently stir each glass with a cocktail stirrer or a spoon to mix the tea syrup with the sparkling juice.
8. As an exuberant accent, adorn each portion with a sprig of recently harvested mint and an orange slice rimmed thereon.

VALENTINE'S ROSE AND CHOCOLATE ELIXIR

Immerse yourself in the romance of Valentine's Day with this luxurious Rose and Chocolate Elixir. The enticing aroma of rose petals melds perfectly with the rich depth of chocolate, creating an enchanting beverage that captures the essence of love and celebration. Perfect for sipping alongside your sweetheart or as an indulgent treat to warm the heart.

2 servings　15 minutes　10 minutes

Equipment: Small saucepan, Fine mesh strainer, Measuring cups and spoons

Ingredients:
- 2 cups water
- two black tea sachets (or two teaspoons of black loose-leaf tea)
- 1/4 cup dried rose petals, edible and organic
- 1/4 cup heavy cream
- 3 tbsp semi-sweet chocolate, finely chopped
- 2 tbsp sugar, or to taste
- 1/2 tsp vanilla extract
- optional garnish: whipped cream and a sprinkle of dried rose petals

Directions:
1. Establish a gentle simmer in a small saucepan over 2 cups of water to begin.
2. Once the water is simmering, remove from heat and add black tea bags and dried rose petals, letting them steep for about 5 minutes. The tea should take on a delicate pink hue and rose fragrance.
3. In the meantime, place the finely chopped semi-sweet chocolate in a heat-proof bowl.
4. Pour the hot tea over the grated chocolate after removing the tea leaves and rose petals with a fine mesh strainer after the tea has steeped. Ensure the chocolate is fully melted and the mixture is smooth by continuing to stir.
5. Return the saucepan to the stove at low heat and pour the tea and chocolate mixture back into the pan. Add sugar and vanilla extract, and whisk to combine.
6. Stir in the heavy cream, warming the elixir gently. Be sure to avoid boiling. Heat until it is at your desired temperature, stirring occasionally.
7. Remove from the heat and pour the elixir into two teacups.

MOTHER'S DAY FLORAL BOUQUET TEA

As gentle and endearing as a mother's embrace, this Mother's Day Floral Bouquet Tea is a delicate blend that captures the essence of affection with its floral notes and soft aroma. Celebrate the heart of the family with a cup of tea that's as warm and loving as her spirit.

Equipment: Tea kettle, Teapot, Fine-mesh strainer (optional), Teacups

Ingredients:
- 6 cups filtered water
- 4 tbsp loose leaf white tea
- 2 tbsp dried rose petals
- 2 tbsp dried chamomile flowers
- 1 tbsp dried lavender
- 1 tsp honey, or to taste (optional)
- edible flowers for garnish (such as pansies or marigolds)

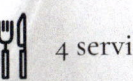

4 servings
10 minutes
5 minutes

Tea Delight

Directions:
1. Heat the filtered water in a tea kettle until it reaches about 175°F (80°C) - white tea is best brewed with water that's not boiling to preserve its delicate flavors.
2. Place the loose leaf white tea, dried rose petals, dried chamomile flowers, and dried lavender into the teapot.
3. Pour out the hot water into the teapot over the tea blend and let it steep for 4-5 minutes. This allows the flavors to meld and the essence of the flowers to infuse into the water.
4. While the tea is steeping, prepare the teacups.
5. After steeping, if desired, pour the tea through a fine-mesh strainer into each cup to remove the tea leaves and flower petals.
6. Taste the tea, and if a touch of sweetness is desired, add a teaspoon of honey and stir gently.
7. Garnish each cup with edible flowers to emphasize the floral theme and add vibrancy to the presentation.

FATHER'S DAY BOLD BREAKFAST BLEND

Celebrate Father's Day with a robust, energizing cup of tea that's as strong and reliable as he is. This Bold Breakfast Blend combines the full-bodied flavors of Assam and Ceylon with a surprising hint of Lapsang Souchong for a smoky finish, perfect for kick-starting a special day with your dad.

4 servings   10 minutes   5 minutes

Equipment: Teapot, Measuring spoons, Kettle, Tea cups

Ingredients:
- 2 tbsp assam black tea leaves
- 2 tbsp ceylon black tea leaves
- 1/2 tsp lapsang souchong tea leaves
- 4 cups freshly boiled water
- optional: milk or sweetener to taste

Directions:
1. To commence, heat the water to a rapid simmer.
2. Measure and combine the Assam, Ceylon, and Lapsang Souchong tea leaves into the teapot.
3. Pour the water into the teapot containing the tea leaves once it has come to a simmer.
4. Permit the tea to infuse for four to five minutes, contingent upon the desired strength of the beverage. The longer it steeps, the more robust the flavor becomes.
5. While the tea steeps, warm up the tea cups with a bit of boiling water if desired, then discard the water.
6. After steeping, strain the tea into warmed cups.
7. If desired, add milk or a sweetener of your choice to enhance the flavor.

HALLOWEEN SPOOKY SPEARMINT BREW

As dusk settles on All Hallows' Eve, conjure up a cauldron of Halloween Spooky Spearmint Brew to bewitch your taste buds and enliven the spirits. This mystifying concoction brings together the freshness of spearmint with the haunting sweetness of licorice and the ethereal glow of butterfly pea flower tea, resulting in an eerie, color-changing potion perfect for your ghoulish gathering

Equipment: Teapot with infuser, Kettle, Fine-mesh strainer, Heat-resistant glasses

6 servings

15 minutes

10 minutes

Ingredients:
- 6 cups filtered water
- 1/4 cup fresh spearmint leaves, plus extra for garnish
- 3 tbsp dried butterfly pea flowers
- 2 licorice root sticks, broken into pieces
- 2 tbsp honey, or to taste
- 1 lemon, sliced into wedges
- edible glitter (gold or silver), for a magical effect (optional)

Sip Slowly

Directions:
1. Place dried butterfly pea flowers into the infuser of your teapot.
2. In a kettle, bring the water just to a boil, then pour it over the butterfly pea flowers. Steep for 5 minutes to unlock the deep blue hue.
3. Add the spearmint leaves and licorice root pieces to the infuser with the butterfly pea flowers, and steep for an additional 5 minutes.
4. After the tea has steeped, remove the infuser or strain the mixture into heat-resistant glasses to remove all the solids.
5. Stir honey into each glass according to personal sweetness preferences.
6. In each glass, strain a wedge of lemon just prior to serving. As the acidity of the lemon reacts with the butterfly pea blossoms, observe as the tea transforms from an eerie blue hue to a vivid, eerie purple.
7. If using, sprinkle a pinch of edible glitter on top of each brew for a mesmerizing, magical sparkle.

THANKSGIVING CRANBERRY-APPLE INFUSION

This Thanksgiving Cranberry-Apple Infusion is the perfect accompaniment to your festive feast. A warm and comforting beverage, it combines the tangy zest of cranberries with the sweet, mellow notes of apple for a drink that embodies the spirit of the season. Garnished with a cinnamon stick, it's like fall in a cup, perfect for sipping around the fireplace with loved ones.

4 servings   15 minutes   10 minutes

Equipment: Medium Saucepan, Fine Mesh Strainer, Heatproof Jug or Pitcher

Ingredients:
- 4 cups water
- 1/2 cup fresh cranberries
- 2 medium apples, cored and sliced
- 2 cinnamon sticks
- 4 whole cloves
- 2 tbsp honey, or to taste
- 4 black tea bags (optional for a caffeinated version)

Directions:
1. In a medium saucepan, bring the water to a gentle simmer. Add the cranberries, apples, cinnamon sticks, and cloves to the hot water.
2. Leave the mixture to simmer for about 5 minutes, until the fruit begins to soften and the water takes on a rich, pink-red color from the cranberries.
3. Stir in the honey while reducing the heat; ensure that it is entirely dissolved. Add the tea bags at this time, remove from the heat, and infuse for three to five minutes, depending on your preferred strength of tea.
4. If desired, remove the tea bags and transfer the infusion to a heatproof container or pitcher via a fine mesh strainer, ensuring that the solids are eliminated.
5. Serve the infusion warm in mugs or tea glasses. For an extra touch of festivity, garnish each serving with a fresh cinnamon stick or a few floating cranberries.

CHRISTMAS EVE PEPPERMINT TWIST

Capture the magic of the season with this festively flavorful "Christmas Eve Peppermint Twist." Perfect for savoring on a chilly December night, this whimsical blend weaves together the classic comfort of black tea with the quintessential holiday flavors of peppermint and cinnamon. Its enchanting aroma alone is enough to summon memories of merriment and cheer around the fireplace.

Equipment: Teapot, Measuring spoons, Mugs, Stirring spoon

Ingredients:
- 4 teaspoons black tea leaves
- 4 cups boiling water
- 4 peppermint candy canes
- 4 cinnamon sticks
- 1/2 cup milk
- 4 tablespoons whipped cream
- 1 teaspoon crushed peppermint or peppermint sprinkles for garnish

4 servings
10 minutes
5 minutes

Enjoy yourself

Directions:
1. Begin by heating the water to a rolling boil. Once ready, pour it into the teapot over the black tea leaves.
2. The tea should steep for three to five minutes, contingent upon the desired potency.
3. While the tea is steeping, insert one minty peppermint candy cane into each mug for a sweet stir of peppermint flavor.
4. Warm the milk over low heat in a small saucepan or in the microwave until it's nice and hot but not boiling.
5. As soon as the tea is steeped to your liking, divide it equally among the candy cane-adorned mugs.
6. Gently pour the hot milk into each mug of tea, giving it a creamy twist.
7. Stir the tea with the candy cane until it gives off a mild peppermint flavor and a hint of sweetness.
8. For an additional dash of Christmas charm, garnish each mug with a dollop of whipped cream and a sprinkle of crushed peppermint or peppermint sprinkles.
9. Don't forget to serve each cup with a cinnamon stick, both for the festive presentation and to swirl for additional spice.

EASTER MORNING HONEY-LEMON GREEN TEA

Wake up to the warmth and cheer of spring with this refreshing Easter Morning Honey-Lemon Green Tea. An uplifting blend of natural sweetness and zesty lemon complements the earthy tones of green tea, creating the perfect beverage to enjoy with family and friends on a joyous Easter morning.

4 servings
5 minutes
10 minutes

Equipment: Teapot or saucepan, Fine-mesh strainer, Measuring spoons, Teacups

Ingredients:
- 4 cups purified water
- 2 tbsp green tea leaves or 4 green tea bags
- 4 tbsp honey, or to taste
- 1 organic lemon, juiced and zest grated
- optional: fresh mint leaves for garnish

Directions:
1. Bring the purified water to just shy of boiling in a teapot or saucepan.
2. Green tea leaves or tea bags should be added to the heated water. If using tea leaves, add directly to the pot, but if using tea bags, place one in each serving cup.
3. Steep the tea for three to four minutes. Adjust the time to taste preference for tea strength.
4. While the tea is steeping, thoroughly wash the lemon. Grate the zest and set aside, then slice the lemon in half and juice it, removing any seeds.
5. Once the tea has steeped, the tea bags or leaves should be removed from the water. Stir in the honey until it is entirely dissolved.
6. For an additional citrusy aroma, incorporate freshly strained lemon juice and lemon zest into the tea mixture.
7. Strain the tea into individual teacups. If used, remove the tea bags without squeezing them, to avoid releasing any bitterness.
8. Preferential: Adorn each cup with a sprig of recently harvested mint to introduce a splash of vibrancy and invigoration.

75

FOURTH OF JULY STAR-SPANGLED COOLER

Celebrate Independence Day with a refreshing, patriotic tea cooler that's as visually striking as fireworks in the summer sky. This vibrant, berry-infused iced tea dazzles with layers of red, white, and blue, offering a cool respite from the warm July festivities. Perfect for barbecues, picnics, and poolside gatherings, this non-alcoholic drink is a crowd-pleaser for all ages.

Equipment: Pitcher, Long Spoon, Ice Cube Trays, Glasses

Ingredients:
- 8 cups cold water
- 6 bags hibiscus or berry tea
- 1/2 cup blueberries, fresh or frozen
- 1/2 cup strawberries, freshly sliced
- 1/4 cup granulated sugar (optional or to taste)
- 1 lime, sliced into thin rounds
- sparkling water (for a fizzy twist, optionally)
- blue and red food coloring (optional, for distinct layers)
- ice cubes (regular or infused with edible blue and red flowers for an added festive touch)

8 servings
20 minutes
0 minutes

Tea Time

Directions:
1. Transfer the tea sachets to a pitcher containing ice-cold water. Refrigerate the tea for two to four hours, or until the desired potency is achieved.
2. While the tea is steeping, prepare your star-shaped ice cubes by placing an edible flower in each mold, fill with water, and freeze—this step is optional, regular ice cubes will work as well.
3. Remove the tea bags from the pitcher after steeping. If you would like a sweeter drink, dissolve the granulated sugar into the tea while it is still lukewarm.
4. Add the lime slices, blueberries, and strawberries to the pitcher. If using food coloring, divide the tea into three separate containers and dye one with a few drops of red food coloring, one with blue, and leave one as is for the white. Chill all separately.
5. When ready to serve, begin by filling each glass with red ice cubes or regular ice. Slowly pour the red tea over, filling the glass about one-third full.
6. Gently add the white layer by pouring regular iced tea slowly over the back of a spoon to minimize mixing.
7. Finish with the blue tea in the same manner to create the blue top layer.
8. If desired for a frozen treat, blend some of the fruit-infused tea with additional ice and layer in the same manner.

HANUKKAH BLUEBERRY BLISS

Celebrate Hanukkah with this warm and joyous Hanukkah Blueberry Bliss tea. Inspired by the Festival of Lights, this tea melds the comforting flavors of winter with the brightness of fresh blueberries, symbolizing the miracle of the oil that burned for eight nights. It's the perfect beverage to sip while enjoying the menorah's glow and indulging in a game of dreidel.

4 servings   10 minutes   5 minutes

Equipment: Teapot or saucepan, Strainer, Measuring cups and spoons

Ingredients:
- 4 cups water
- 4 bags green tea
- 1/2 cup fresh blueberries, plus extra for garnish
- 2 tbsp honey, or to taste
- 1 cinnamon stick
- 1 tbsp lemon juice
- zest of 1/2 lemon
- fresh mint leaves for garnish (optional)

Directions:
1. Bring the water to a boil in a teapot or saucepan.
2. Once the water has boiled, add the green tea bags and steep for 3 minutes, then remove the tea bags.
3. In a separate bowl, lightly crush the 1/2 cup of blueberries, releasing their juice.
4. Add the crushed blueberries, along with the honey, cinnamon stick, lemon juice, and zest to the tea. Stir well to combine.
5. Reduce the heat and simmer the mixture for about 5 minutes to allow the flavors to infuse.
6. Remove the tea from heat. Pour through a strainer into cups or a serving pot to remove the blueberry skins and cinnamon stick.
7. Garnish each cup with a few fresh blueberries and, if you like, a mint leaf for a refreshing touch.

76

DIWALI SPICED SAFFRON TEA

Celebrate the Festival of Lights with this aromatic Diwali Spiced Saffron Tea. Saffron, the most precious spice in the world, lends this beverage a golden hue and a rich, exotic flavor that pairs beautifully with the warming spices. This beverage is ideal for communal consumption with cherished ones on Diwali or any auspicious autumn evening.

Equipment: Medium saucepan, Fine-mesh strainer, Teapot

Ingredients:
- 4 cups water
- 2-inch piece fresh ginger, sliced
- 4-5 strands saffron
- 4 green cardamom pods, lightly crushed
- 2 cloves
- 1 small cinnamon stick
- 4 tsp black tea leaves or 4 black tea bags
- honey or sugar, to taste
- milk or non-dairy alternative (optional), to taste
- sliced almonds or pistachios for garnish (optional)

4 servings

5 minutes

10 minutes

Zen Sip

Directions:
1. Hydrogenate water in a medium saucepan while incorporating the cinnamon stick, cardamom capsules, saffron, and cardamom. Simmer the water for five minutes to impart the flavors of the seasonings.
2. Add the black tea leaves to the spiced water and simmer for another 5 minutes on low heat. If you prefer a stronger tea, allow it to brew for a few additional minutes.
3. Strain the tea into a serving pitcher or teapot to eliminate the solids after removing the saucepan from the heat.
4. Honey or sugar should be added until the desired sweetness is achieved. For a more creamy consistency, a small amount of milk or a suitable non-dairy substitute may be added to flavor.
5. Serve the spiced saffron tea in individual cups, garnished with a sprinkle of sliced almonds or pistachios if desired.

MIDSUMMER NIGHT'S DREAM HERBAL MIX

Immerse yourself in the enchantment of a midsummer evening with this soothing, floral blend that perfectly captures the magic of the season's most whimsical night. This caffeine-free herbal mix combines the gentle notes of chamomile with a hint of citrus zest and a whisper of mint, making it ideal for unwinding after a day soaking up the summer sun.

4 servings   10 minutes   10 minutes

Equipment: Teapot, Strainer, Kettle

Ingredients:
- 4 cups purified water
- 2 tbsp dried chamomile flowers
- 1 tbsp fresh mint leaves
- 1 tsp lemon balm leaves
- 1 tsp rose petals, edible and organic
- peel of 1/2 orange, avoid the pith for less bitterness
- 1 tbsp honey (optional, to taste)
- edible flowers for garnish (optional)

Directions:
1. Bring the purified water to a boil in a kettle.
2. While the water is warming, place the dried chamomile flowers, fresh mint leaves, lemon balm, and rose petals into the teapot.
3. After the water has heated to a boil, promptly remove it from the heat and allow it to settle for an additional minute. You want the water hot but not scalding, to preserve the delicate flavor of the herbs.
4. Pour the hot water over the herbal mix in the teapot. Add the orange peel on top.
5. Cover the teapot and let it steep for 7-10 minutes, depending on your preference for strength.
6. If you desire a bit of sweetness, stir honey into the hot tea until it dissolves.
7. Strain the tea into cups, ensuring that none of the herbs or the orange peel make it into the serving.
8. Incorporate edible blossoms as a garnish to evoke the aesthetic allure of midsummer nights.

AUTUMN EQUINOX CIDER SPICE TEA

As the leaves change and the days shorten, warm up with a cup of Autumn Equinox Cider Spice Tea. This festive concoction blends the crispness of fresh apple cider with the warming notes of cinnamon, clove, and star anise, perfectly capturing the essence of autumn in a mug. A subtle undertone of black tea provides a comforting base, making this beverage a delightful treat to savor the balance of light and dark on the equinox.

Equipment: Large saucepan, Fine-mesh strainer, Measuring cups and spoons

Ingredients:
- 4 cups apple cider
- 2 black tea bags or 2 tsp loose-leaf black tea
- 2 cinnamon sticks
- 4 whole cloves
- 2 star anise
- 1 orange, sliced
- optional sweetener (honey, sugar, or maple syrup) to taste
- optional garnish: apple slices or cinnamon stick

4 servings | 10 minutes | 15 minutes

Directions:
1. Combine the apple cider, cinnamon sticks, whole cloves, and star anise in a large saucepan.
2. Over medium heat, bring the mixture to a low simmer while allowing the seasonings to infuse for approximately 5 minutes.
3. Add the black tea bags or loose-leaf black tea (in a tea infuser) to the saucepan, along with the orange slices.
4. Continue to simmer gently for an additional 5 minutes, ensuring the flavors meld without bringing the mixture to a boil.
5. After 5 minutes, remove from heat and allow to steep for a more pronounced flavor profile. Amid this period, the tea's essence will assume a prominent role.
6. Use a fine-mesh strainer to filter out the spices and tea leaves (if using loose-leaf) into a heat-proof pitcher or jug.
7. If a sweeter taste is desired, add your choice of sweetener and stir until dissolved.
8. Pour the Autumn Equinox Cider Spice Tea into individual mugs.
9. If preferred, garnish with a fresh apple slice or an additional cinnamon stick in each mug.

Tea Delight

WINTER SOLSTICE GINGERBREAD TEA

Immerse yourself in the cozy comfort of wintertime with this Winter Solstice Gingerbread Tea. Celebrate the shortest day of the year with the rich aromas of ginger, cinnamon, and molasses – reminiscent of freshly-baked gingerbread cookies. This enticing blend will warm your soul and infuse your home with festive cheer.

4 servings | 10 minutes | 15 minutes

Equipment: Medium Saucepan, Mesh Strainer, Teapot or Serving Jug

Ingredients:
- 4 cups water
- 4 black tea bags or 4 tbsp loose black tea
- 2 cinnamon sticks
- 1-inch fresh ginger, thinly sliced
- 4 whole cloves
- 2 star anise
- 1/4 tsp ground nutmeg
- 1/4 cup molasses
- milk or a milk alternative, to taste
- whipped cream (optional, for serving)
- gingerbread cookies (crumbled, for garnish)

Directions:
1. Bring the water to a boil in a medium saucepan containing the water.
2. Once boiling, add the black tea, cinnamon sticks, sliced ginger, whole cloves, star anise, and ground nutmeg to the water.
3. Reduce heat and allow the mixture to simmer for about 10 minutes, so the spices can fully infuse their flavors into the water.
4. Stir in the molasses until it is well-dispersed and fully dissolved into the brew.
5. Remove from heat and let the tea steep for an additional 5 minutes to develop a strong, spicy flavor.
6. Meanwhile, warm your teapot or serving jug with some hot water and then discard the water.
7. Place the mesh strainer over the teapot or serving jug and pour the tea through it to catch the spices and tea leaves.
8. Serve the tea in individual cups and add milk or a milk substitute to taste.
9. Optional: Top each cup with a dollop of whipped cream and crumbled gingerbread cookies for an extra festive and indulgent touch.

SPRING RENEWAL DETOX BLEND

As the days warm and flowers bloom, refresh and cleanse your body with the Spring Renewal Detox Blend, perfect for celebrating the turn of the season. This invigorating tea blend draws upon nature's finest herbs renowned for their detoxifying properties, offering a delightful symphony of flavors that will rejuvenate your spirit and awaken your senses.

Equipment: Teapot, Mesh Strainer or Tea Infuser, Teacups

Ingredients:
- 4 cups purified water
- 2 tbsp green tea leaves
- 1 tbsp fresh mint leaves
- 1 tsp dandelion leaves, chopped
- 1 tsp nettle leaves, dried
- 1 tsp burdock root, dried and sliced
- 1 tsp lemon zest
- honey or maple syrup, to taste (optional)
- a few fresh edible flowers (such as violets or rose petals) for garnish

4 servings

10 minutes

10 minutes

Sip Slowly

Directions:
1. Bring the purified water to a just below boiling in a kettle.
2. Place the green tea leaves, mint, dandelion leaves, nettle leaves, and burdock root into the teapot's infuser.
3. Once the water is heated, pour it over the tea mixture in the pot.
4. Allow the mix to steep for 5 to 7 minutes, depending on your desired strength of the tea.
5. While the tea is steeping, grate the lemon zest finely.
6. After steeping the tea, add the lemon zest to the teapot, stirring gently.
7. Let the blend sit for another 1-2 minutes to allow the zest to release its oils and aroma.
8. Carefully strain the tea into individual teacups using the mesh strainer if not using an infuser.
9. Sweeten with honey or maple syrup if a touch of sweetness is desired.
10. Garnish each cup with a few fresh edible flowers to elevate the visual appeal and emphasize the theme of renewal.

ANNIVERSARY ROMANTIC RED ROOIBOS

Celebrate love and togetherness with the Anniversary Romantic Red Rooibos. This heartwarming cup pairs the naturally sweet and nutty flavors of red rooibos with the enchanting fragrance of roses and the warmth of vanilla. It's the perfect tea to reflect on cherished memories and create new ones.

2 servings   10 minutes   5 minutes

Equipment: Teapot with infuser, Measuring spoons, Kettle

Ingredients:
- 1 1/2 tbsp red rooibos leaves
- 2 cups filtered water
- 1 tsp dried rose petals, edible
- 1/2 vanilla bean, scraped or 1 tsp pure vanilla extract
- 2 tsp honey, or to taste
- a small pinch of pink himalayan salt
- optional: fresh rose petals for garnish
- optional: 2 tbsp rosewater for an enhanced rose flavor

Directions:
1. Bring the filtered water to a temperature just below boiling (approximately 200°F or 95°C).
2. Place the red rooibos leaves and dried rose petals into the infuser of your teapot.
3. Pour the hot water over the rooibos and rose petals, then add the scraped vanilla bean or vanilla extract and the pinch of Pink Himalayan salt.
4. While the tea steeps for five minutes under the cover of the teapot, the flavors will harmonise, resulting in a cup that is both delicate and romantic in nature.
5. After 5 minutes, remove the infuser to avoid over-steeping, which can cause bitterness.
6. Stir in the honey until dissolved, adjusting the sweetness to your liking. If using rosewater, add it now for a more pronounced rose flavor.
7. Serve the tea in your favorite cups and garnish with fresh rose petals, if desired.

Conclusion

As we reach the end of our journey through "Ultimate Tea Recipe Book: Over 100+ Masterful Recipes for the Modern Tea Lover," we hope that you have discovered not just the rich variety and depth that tea offers, but also the joy and creativity in crafting each cup. From the energizing morning blends in "Breakfast Teas: Energize Your Morning" to the soothing concoctions in "Evening Teas: Unwind and Relax," this book has aimed to explore the vast world of tea in all its forms. We've delved into traditional classics, modern twists, and innovative creations, ensuring there's something for every palate and occasion.

Now that you are equipped with over 100 masterful tea recipes and the knowledge about their origins, health benefits, and preparation methods, we encourage you to put this information into practice. Experiment with these recipes, tweak them to your taste, and maybe even create your own unique blends. Remember, each cup of tea is a personal journey and an expression of your individuality.

If you found this book helpful and enjoyable, we would be grateful if you could take a moment to leave a review on Amazon. Your feedback is not only immensely valuable to us but also helps fellow tea enthusiasts discover and explore the wonderful world of tea. Let's continue to spread the love and appreciation for this timeless beverage.

Thank you for accompanying us on this flavorful adventure. May your teacup always be full, and may each brew bring you joy, health, and a moment of tranquility. Happy brewing!

Index

A

After-Dinner Anise Comfort 53
Anniversary Romantic Red Rooibos 79
Apple Cinnamon Morning Energizer 44
Apricot Orchard Oolong 36
Artisanal Bergamot and Rose Hip Blend 66
Autumn Equinox Cider Spice Tea 78
Autumn Harvest Pumpkin Chai 71

B

Bergamot Bliss Herbal Tisane 40
Berry Blast White Tea Infusion 31
Bold Breakfast Pu-erh 34
Bold Masala Chai for Spicy Cuisine 58

C

Caramel Whisper Black Tea 40
Caramelized Honey Rooibos for Comforting Evenings 68
Cardamom and Clove Morning Tea 33
Celestial Lemon Balm Calm 49
Cherry Blossom Sencha 42
Christmas Eve Peppermint Twist 75
Citrus Burst Darjeeling for Seafood 64
Citrus Harmony Earl Grey 38
Cozy Clove and Cocoa Tisane 55

D

Decaf Ceylon Solace 49
Delicate White Peony for Light Dishes 59
Diwali Spiced Saffron Tea 77
Dream Weaver's Wild Berry Brew 56
Dusk Delight Passionflower 51

E

Earl Grey with a Twist of Bergamot 27
Easter Morning Honey-Lemon Green Tea 75
Elegant Jasmine Harmony for Asian Fare 60
Evening Rose Hip Serenade 48

F

Father's Day Bold Breakfast Blend 73
Fennel and Anise Digestif Herbal Tea 67
Festive Winter Spice Tea 70
Floral Hibiscus Bliss for Tropical Meals 63
Floral Symphony Rose Tea 37
Fourth of July Star-Spangled Cooler 76
Fragrant Lemongrass and Basil Tisane 66

G

Ginger Peach Tea Sparkler 44
Ginseng and Green Tea Power Brew 32
Golden Chrysanthemum Brew 42
Golden Turmeric and Black Pepper Tea 30

H

Halloween Spooky Spearmint Brew 74
Hanukkah Blueberry Bliss 76
Hearty Roasted Oolong for Grilled Foods 60
Honey Vanilla Rooibos Delight 29

I

Invigorating Lemongrass Mate 32

J

Jasmine Dawn Elixir 30
Jasmine Jewel Green Tea 41

L

Lavender Breeze Chamomile Infusion 36
Lemon Verbena and Thyme Tonic 43
Lively Lemon Ginger Detox Tea 27

M

Matcha Energy Booster 28
Midsummer Night's Dream Herbal Mix 77
Milky Way Warm Cinnamon Infusion 51

Mint Awakening Herbal Blend 26
Mint Medley Green Tea 38
Moonlight Chamomile Dream 47
Morning Energizer Darjeeling Tea 39
Morning Glory Green Tea 25
Moroccan Mint and Licorice Tea 45
Mother's Day Floral Bouquet Tea 73

N
New Year's Sparkling Tea Toast 72
Nightfall Valerian Whisper 50

P
Peaceful Peppermint and Licorice 54
Peach Perfection White Tea 37
Peppermint Pick-Me-Up 29
Pomegranate Panache Black Tea 33

Q
Quiet Time Tangerine Blend 55

R
Raspberry Hibiscus Cooler 39
Refreshing Fennel and Green Tea Blend 34
Refreshing Mint and Cucumber Green Tea 62
Restful Rooibos Retreat 52
Rich Lapsang Souchong Smoky Blend 58
Robust Yunnan Black Tea for Rich Foods 63

S
Savory Sage Green Tea 59
Serene Sage and Honey Hush 53
Sleepy Thyme Embrace 56
Slumbering Lotus Steep 54
Smoked Cherry Wood Black Tea 65
Soothing Lavender Grey for After-Dinner Relaxation 64
Sophisticated Earl Grey for European Cuisine 61
Spice Market Herbal Infusion 65
Spiced Assam Chai 26
Spiced Orange Rooibos 43
Spring Cherry Blossom Celebration 70
Spring Renewal Detox Blend 79
Starlight Mint Melody 48

Summer Berry Sangria Tea 41
Summer Solstice Iced Berry Blend 71
Sundown Spiced Vanilla 50
Sunrise Citrus Black Tea 25
Sweet Cinnamon Oolong Revival 28
Sweet Lychee Black Tea for Dessert Pairing 67

T
Thanksgiving Cranberry-Apple Infusion 74
Tranquil Tulsi and Orange 52
Twilight Lavender Soothe 47

V
Valentine's Rose and Chocolate Elixir 72
Vanilla Orchid Black Tea for Sophisticated Palates 68
Vanilla Orchid Oolong 45

W
Warming Cinnamon Pu-erh 62
Winter Solstice Gingerbread Tea 78

Z
Zesty Lemon-Ginger Detox for Cleansing 61
Zesty Orange Pekoe Punch 31

Printed in Great Britain
by Amazon